"*Pursuing Wild Trout* is a true celebration of the wild trout and wild places that haunt our fishing dreams. Bob Madgic has shared a lifetime of angling passion, and has infused it with his own deep commitment to wilderness conservation. A conservation-minded angler cannot help but come away from this book with a renewed dedication to protecting the fragile habitat that wild trout and salmon depend on."
    —Charles F. Gauvin, President and CEO, **Trout Unlimited.**

"*Pursuing Wild Trout: A Journey in Wilderness Values* is a wonderfully rich book, as lyrical, exuberant, and vivid as the rivers themselves. Bob Madgic celebrates the life of rivers, the countless opportunities to enjoy them, and the tireless crusades to save them. This book belongs in the library of everyone who loves the out-of-doors."
    —Betsy Reifsnider, Executive Director, **Friends of the River.**

"Wild rivers and wild trout are inseparable. *Pursuing Wild Trout* chronicles a passion for exploring and protecting the wild rivers that are necessary both for trout and the quality of our own lives."
    —Rebecca Wodder, President, *American Rivers.*

"*Pursuing Wild Trout* is a lesson about interconnectedness: spiritual, physical and ecological. Bob Madgic makes the connections that need to be made. And he holds up a mirror to us in the conservation world, reminding us to remember, strengthen and rely upon that interconnectedness in our own lives."
    —John C. Sawhill, President and CEO, **The Nature Conservancy.**

"Bob Madgic treats the reader to a banquet of sumptuous sights, sounds and reflections from years of chasing wilderness trout around California and the world. He does a wonderful job of distilling his adventures down into a series of values: ethical statements personally absorbed from years in the field. In doing so, Bob Madgic gets at the heart of our sport, and his words aren't 'barbless' either. They stick with you."

    —Chip O'Brien, Author of *River Journal: The Sacramento River.*

"Bob Madgic is a born explorer, with a knack for finding untrammeled terrain and an obvious love for all things wild."

    —Richard Anderson, Editor, ***California Fly Fisher*** magazine.

"*Pursuing Wild Trout* offers a textured look into the world of back roads, wilderness trails, and native trout as bright as jewels. It's a world that never ceases to beckon and delight us."

    —Nick Lyons, author, publisher, **Nick Lyons Books.**

"Bob Madgic's love of the wilderness and the trout that grow there comes through in every word of this book."

    —Bill Sunderland, outdoor writer and author of *California Blue Ribbon Trout Streams.*

"*Pursuing Wild Trout* is about places, thoughts, and things dear to my heart. I'm sure it will touch a similar nerve in many readers."

    —Ralph Cutter, ***California School of Fly Fishing.***

"The metamorphosis of an angler to an environmentalist is as clear to the reader as the trout streams Bob Madgic has fallen hopelessly in love with. It will become obvious to anyone reading this book that there is common sense, simplistic beauty and astute wisdom in using wild trout as the barometer of watershed health."

    —Jim Edmundson, Executive Director, ***California Trout.***

PURSUING WILD TROUT

A Journey in Wilderness Values

BY

BOB MADGIC

Illustrated by William Crary

River Bend Books

ISBN 0-9660743-1-9

Library of Congress Catalog Number: 97- 092758

The William O. Douglas quote was taken from *My Wilderness* by William O. Douglas, 1960, © William O. Douglas, reprinted by permission of the estate of William O. Douglas.

Excerpts from *Siddhartha* are reprinted by permission of New Directions Publishing Corporation.

The Wallace Stegner quote is reprinted by permission of the Stegner family.

Parts of chapters in this book have been previously published in *California Fly Fisher*.

Published by:

River Bend Books

6412 Clear View Dr.

Anderson, CA 96007

Phone: (530) 365-5852

CONTENTS

Acknowledgments

When I started writing this book, I expected to finish it in six months. Instead it took four years. Although I alone am responsible for whatever flaws it may possess, I am greatly indebted to the following individuals who generously responded to my calls for help.

First and foremost, I wish to acknowledge the efforts of my longtime friend, Jack Hamilton. At a crucial stage he meticulously reviewed each chapter, and the organization of the book as a whole, providing many editorial suggestions. I am most grateful to him.

Persons who read parts of the manuscript and passed on to me helpful comments include: Tom Jennings, Richard Keady, Ruth Rowe, Bob Wetzel, Marilyn Young, Paul Sakamoto, Mike Pease, Stuart Brewster, Bill Kaufmann, Richard Bruce, Jim Mongillo, Dick Stark and Tom Watkins.

Ralph Cutter reviewed an early draft of the manuscript and provided me with insightful comments that caused me to make several strategic revisions. Richard Anderson offered editorial suggestions that prompted some last minute changes.

Leslie Crowe, Archivist for the Bank of Stockton Archives, helped me with historical background on the central Sierra. Howard C. Lewis provided me with material on a subject dear to his heart—Monte Wolf.

I received critical assistance on clarifying items relating to ecosystems and species interdependence from: Dr. Robert Behnke, Department of Fishery and Wildlife Biology, Colorado State University; Dr. Bert Cushing, stream ecologist; Dr. Peter Moyle, Department of Wildlife, Fish, and Conservation Biology at the University of California at Davis; and Harry Rectenwald, California Department of Fish and Game Office at Redding.

On matters involving habitat and the spotted owl I received help from: Professor Rocky Gutierrez, Department of Wildlife Management, Humboldt State University at Arcata; Dr. Lee Fitzhugh, Department of Wildlife, Fish, and Conservation Biology at the University of California at Davis; and Vincent Muehter of the National Audubon Society.

Johanna Thomas, Executive Director of the Tuolumne River Preservation Trust, Bob Kinkead, Jim Crouse, and Bob Wetzel of the Calaveras Ranger District of the Stanislaus National Forest in Hathaway Pines, helped me in compiling the pictorial section of the book. I also want to extend my deepest thanks to William Crary who enhanced the book with his many talents in design and illustration, and his love of nature.

I am very indebted to all of those companions who joined me in the outdoor experiences that provided the basis for this book. I especially want to mention Jim Vettel, Jim Rowe, Bud West, and Dick Minetti, now deceased.

Lastly, the persons who were with me in every step of my journey, and who always will be, are my beloved wife, Diane, and our wonderful children, Jennifer, Kirk and Doug. With love and devotion to each, I dedicate this book to them.

Prologue

A few years ago I told a close friend that I don't keep the trout I catch. "Why do you fish, then?" she inquired.

I responded with the words that first came to mind. "I enjoy fishing as a sport. You like to play tennis, I like to fish. It's a way to experience the outdoors."

My words, though, didn't express what fishing truly means to me. I could feel the deeper answers to my friend's question inside of me, but I couldn't put them into words. How do I communicate that I am pulled to this endeavor like nothing else in my life. That when I fish, I feel fulfilled. That I see in a river's currents and depths life's mysteries. That fishing for wild trout within a wilderness setting clarifies for me what's important in life.

How do I convey these profundities to someone within the context of a sport that many people, including my good friend, probably only see as recreation? Like any sport. Do others find similar meaning when playing golf? Or riding a bike? Or rock climbing? Or canoeing? I suspect some do.

The personal insights I've gained from fishing ventures did not readily happen. It took many outdoor excursions across many years before I came to understand what the pursuit of wild trout and the concept of wilderness have contributed to my life.

While growing up in Connecticut, the pull of the outdoors and the beckoning of fish and water took hold of me early. As a young boy, I would cut a long, thin birch sapling, put string on it, affix a cork bobber, and, usually with my older brother, go searching for a hidden pond that just might hold fish. The kind of water was important—it had to be tucked away in a place that few had visited, an objective helped considerably by often going to fenced reservoirs and other "no trespassing" waters.

Throughout these early years, I possessed little understanding or appreciation for what I eventually came to see as "wilderness values." I kept all of the fish I caught; I attempted to kill any wild creature that crossed my path; I showed little respect for the land; I saw no connections from one creature to the next, or between the integrity of the natural world and my own being. However, whenever I returned from college for a much needed break, the first thing I usually did was to take a walk in the woods, even in the dead of winter with snow all about. In doing so, I would feel the stress draining from my body, and experience the mind healing and spirit enhancement that a wild setting fosters.

Though I took a hiatus from fishing while I attended college, participated in sports, got married, and started raising a family, my attraction to water, fishing and wilderness never ceased. They regained their importance in my life when we had a cabin built in the central Sierra in 1973. Two major rivers systems—the Mokelumne and the Stanislaus—had cut deep canyons on either side of the highway near our cabin, creating opportunities for hiking wilderness trails, fishing hard-to-get-to waters, and rafting wild rivers. My constant and faithful companions throughout these years were my wife Diane, daughter Jennifer, and sons Kirk and Doug.

In time, we searched other rivers—the Tuolumne, the East Carson, the Middle Fork of the Stanislaus, the San Joaquin—for those elusive rewards. We explored remote sections of smaller streams. We traveled across the globe to the rivers of New Zealand. From these explorations, with wild trout the ongoing focus, my love for wild rivers and wild places grew deeper with each passing year. Our wilderness experiences nurtured family togetherness, and a sense of community among a larger network of companions and co-adventurers.

Since that time to the present, I've been engaged in an ongoing search for that hidden stretch of water harboring wild trout, and something more. The answer to my friend's question evolved across many wilderness adventures in the quest for wild trout. When I began this book, my main purpose was simply to describe those adventures and my related fly fishing experiences. But one thing led to another, and I found myself drawing connections, until everything became connected. I slowly realized I was writing about the forces of nature, how nature works, and in effect, my own spiritual growth. For in addition to uncovering the answer to the question, "why fish?", the pursuit of wild trout has led me to the discovery that, in wilderness, one can find life's deepest meanings.

1
More Than A Place: The Mokelumne Wilderness

All mountain streets have streams to thread them, or deep grooves where a stream might run. You would do well to avoid that range uncomforted by singing floods. You will find it forsaken of most things but beauty and madness and death and God—**Mary Austin, The Land of Little Rain**

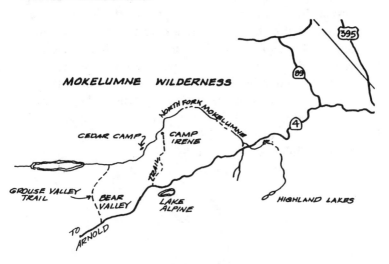

Between Ebbetts Pass (Highway 4) and Carson Pass (Highway 88) in the central Sierra, the North Fork of the Mokelumne River flows through the granite mountains and rich forests making up the Mokelumne Wilderness. Deep in the bowl-shaped canyon, dense stands of pine, fir, and cedar fill three distinct basins connected, by river— Camp Irene, Cedar Camp and Grouse Valley—hike-in destinations for backpackers and anglers. The entire area sits at the foot of Mokelumne Peak, a multicolored, towering summit flanked by jagged volcanic ridges called the Mokelumne Tetons.

The name "Mokelumne" can be traced to a powerful Miwok Indian tribe, the Mo-kel-kos, who dwelled in the

Central Valley near the present town of Lockeford. The Miwoks used the termination "um-na" to refer to a river, thus "Mokelumna" (and "Toulumna," "Cosumna"). These Native Americans left the lowlands each summer to travel to the high country of the North Fork of the Mokelumne, a region teeming with wild animals, birds and fish. It was their "summer place of the gods."

The Washoe tribe from Nevada also visited the area, trading goods with the Miwoks. In the early 1800's, John C. Fremont, Jedediah Smith and Kit Carson were among the first white men to explore this part of the Sierra. After the decline of the Native Americans in the mid-nineteenth century, a few gold seekers, and later, shepherds and livestock tenders, were the principal visitors to the region.

The Mokelumne Wilderness became part of the National Wilderness Preservation System in 1964 with passage of the Federal Wilderness Act. It was expanded to its present size of 105, 165 acres with passage of the California Wilderness Act of 1984.

A Greeting

The best view of the Mokelumne Wilderness is from the slopes of the Bear Valley Ski Area, located between Lake Tahoe and Yosemite National Park. It's where I first saw the canyon in 1973 while maneuvering down the likes of ski runs Groovy Gully, Oopla and Bear Boogie.

When one looks across the gaping canyon to towering Mokelumne Peak with its many pastel hues, one experiences a scene rendering skiing more than a mere sport. Off to the east, massive rock walls encase the North Fork of the Mokelumne River as it slices through the high mountainous terrain and down through the terraced canyon bowl. There, the river alternately crashes down steep drops in pulsating masses of white and flows serenely in long, dark green pools.

12

The wild river almost a vertical mile down seemed beyond reach when I first gazed at it that day in 1973. A descent into the canyon's depths looked formidable. A climb back out looked worse. But months later, a description of the Mokelumne remarking its large-sized trout caught my eye. I began to lay plans.

The Camp Irene Trail down to the river is seven and a half miles, mainly downhill. Not too bad for a family trek, I figured. The return climb out, however, is the steepest part of the Tahoe-To-Yosemite Trail, involving an elevation gain of 3600 feet. This part would require conviction.

Also disconcerting were reports the Mokelumne Wilderness was a rattlesnake pit. Not wanting to place my family in harm's way, I asked a ranger about the chances of meeting up with one of these creatures, and took comfort in hearing rattlesnake sightings are rare. I concluded that their presence would not deter us; it actually added a degree of excitement to a trip.

For an exploratory outing, agreed to by the family, we would leave early morning, spend one or two hours fishing the river, and hike out the same day. Although the schedule involved fifteen miles of strenuous hiking, it eliminated an overnight stay and heavy backpacks.

My kids enjoyed fishing, but my wife had decided, after humoring me the first couple of years of our marriage, that fishing just didn't suit her temperament. Just as well. One or two compulsive fisher-persons per family is probably the best one can hope for. Diane loves the outdoors, sets a mean trail pace, and as a dietitian, always supplies healthy trail food, which I often supplement with junk food.

In early August, we departed from the cabin at 6:15 a.m., and drove up Highway 4 to the base of Mt. Reba and the start of the Camp Irene Trail. We parked our canary yellow Honda in a parking area in an open field, and with Mokelumne Peak glowing from the early morning sun, we started the three-and-a-half-mile ascent on a rocky jeep road to a ridge astride barren Mt. Reba at 8,750 feet in elevation. From the ridge, we would

13

follow the plunging, twisting four-mile route down to Camp Irene and the river.

In an hour and a half, we reached the summit. A large snow field remained on the shady, north slope facing the canyon. After sliding down it, we picked up the trail in a terrain of rock and gravel, sparse, gnarled vegetation and stunted trees.

We had gone less than fifty yards below the snow when Diane, hiking out front, screamed and jumped off the trail. Close behind, the kids and I quickly saw what frightened her— a huge rattlesnake, its head high and poised for a strike, its tail buzzing madly. My wife had stepped right next to the rattler as it lay coiled alongside the trail, probably waiting to ambush a rodent. The startled snake could easily have sunk its fangs into her leg. We were as shocked as it must have been since we never expected to see a rattlesnake at this high an elevation, nor one of this size and girth.

In my youth, I possessed the outdoor ethic of "if-it-moves-kill-it." Squirrels, woodchucks, birds, rabbits, and other creatures of the Connecticut woods all met a harsh fate if I happened by with my trusty 22 rifle, Hollywood images of the old west firmly implanted in my mind. I killed, or tried to kill, every snake I came across. Don't ask me why. So as this monster reptile began retreating down a slight incline, still warning us with its striking pose, I looked for a suitable rock or stick to dispose of it. Before I found one, the rattler slithered into a haven of bushes and trees at the base of the bank.

I circled the snake's sanctuary, listening to the constant hum of its rattles. It occurred to me that this shady spot would not be a good place for a hiker to seek refuge from a hot sun. Thinking its skin would have made quite a trophy, I was disappointed the rattlesnake escaped, estimating its length as at least five feet. However, the excitement of the encounter and quickness with which it ended may have affected my judgment—in more ways than one. As later events would show, this day was destined for further excitement.

Still semi-shocked from our early morning wake-up call, we resumed hiking, alongside a cascading stream, across granite outcroppings, through thick manzanita bushes and stands of willows. After an hour, despite our rapid downhill pace, the canyon bottom still looked a long distance away.

We stopped for snacks where the trail was carved into a hillside, presenting us with a sweeping vista of the lower canyon. To augment the trail food Diane had packed, I passed around a bag of jelly donuts that I had carefully stowed in my daypack, thinking that dried fruit wouldn't sustain a person's needs on this tough hike like a jelly donut. I would worry about clogged arteries later.

The rest and snacks renewed our energy. With most of our hiking still before us, we didn't linger. Another half mile into the death march, Diane halted and said, "Rats, I left the camera behind."

Ordinarily *I* would have gone back, but I figured once we reached the river, Diane could rest while the kids and I fished. Plus she was in the best hiking condition. So while we waited, my wife retraced our route, adding another mile to her day. When she returned, we once again straightened our wobbly legs and allowed gravity to do its thing.

Finally we hit level terrain, but not yet the river. After tramping through a forest of yellow oaks and thick underbrush for another punishing distance, we reached a grove of huge incense cedars, white pines and red firs. Nearby, the North Fork of the Mokelumne River flowed silently through the forest. Camp Irene. My watch showed 11:30.

Despite our weary legs, the kids and I assembled our rods and started fishing. I have never been able to sit by a stream for more than a few minutes without getting my line in the water—the only way to catch anything.

Our bait and spinning lures attracted a half dozen or so scrappy rainbows. Jennifer landed the best—an eleven incher. We broke when Diane signaled that lunch was ready, all spread out on a flat rock. After quickly consuming my peanut butter and jelly sandwich, drink, cookie, and apple, I was off again.

At the tail of a long pool, I spotted three nice fish holding. I called Kirk and told him to drift down a grasshopper. When he did, the biggest trout, around fifteen inches, rose and engulfed the struggling hopper. Kirk pulled back and set the hook, yelling "ya hoo!" as the hefty trout thrashed about the pool, yanking and tugging. Kirk's line suddenly slackened and I glimpsed the rainbow streaking away. A poorly tied knot had come undone.

"Darn it!" Kirk said, throwing his rod down in disgust. As I approached him on the bank, Kirk was fighting back tears. I assured him we would come back and nail that bugger the next time—a promise Kirk would hold me to many times over in ensuing years.

Our six fish cleaned, we packed up, stretched our stiff legs, and started the dreaded seven-and-a-half-mile climb out.

With the sun beating down at us from a cloudless sky, my thoughts focused on the cold beer in the cabin fridge.

A Farewell

Should be back at the cabin by five-thirty, I estimated while walking through the oak woods. First, though, we had a steep mountainside staring down at us that we needed to negotiate.

Where the trail crossed a grassy section alongside a stream, Jennifer screamed, "a snake!" pointing to where I was just about to step. I froze. Right in front of me fully extended was another gigantic reptile, only this five footer had no rattles, thank God. After a few deep breaths to get oxygen back into my brain and settle my nerves, I skirted the creature and fell in line once more, not wanting anyone to know that almost stepping on that thing had scared me half to death.

For the next three hours, it was up, up, up. With the top of the ridge still a quarter mile distant, my aching quadriceps were telling me to call it a day. Diane and the kids were trooping on ahead. In my weariness, I didn't notice that billowy cumulus clouds now covered much of the sky.

The white clouds overhead began turning into dark ones. We pushed on. The sky got darker and darker. Thunder rumbled in the distance. Diane looked concerned. We quickened our pace.

By the time we reached the snow field just below the ridge, black clouds covered the sky overhead. As we neared the top, steaks of lightning and sharp thunder claps rocked the heavens. Off to the west, lightning bolts rattled tree tops.

My wife does not like lightning storms. I'm not that fond of them either, but Diane literally is terrified by lightning. When we camp, she flies out of the tent at the first bolt, and seeks refuge in the car until the storm ends. In fact she may be smarter than I am on this matter.

As the storm grew increasingly fierce, with bolt after bolt crashing toward the earth accompanied by ear-splitting thunder, we were on a high, bare ridge, the most dangerous spot. Diane broke into a run, followed by Kirk, Jen and Doug, all of them desperately trying to outrun the storm. I continued walking, whistling, cocky as usual, unaware my two-piece fly rod was sticking up from my daypack like a lightning rod. We should be safe as long as the bolts stay to the east, I thought.

A lightning bolt streaked the sky to the west placing us right smack in the middle of the storm. I started to run, fly rod now in hand, barely able to keep my balance down the rocky course. Up ahead Diane let out a shriek and fell down. Kirk, running alongside her, thought she was struck by lightning. Fortunately, she had only stumbled on loose rocks, but it was a hard fall. With scraped hands and bruised knees, she got up and continued running.

"Head for the trees!" I yelled.

Panic stricken, we raced to get out of the open terrain, lightning crashing all around us like bomb blasts. Completely at the mercy of unpredictable forces, we scrambled toward the wooded area, our legs finding strength where none existed moments earlier.

With no pause in the thunder and lightning, we reached the grove of trees, one mile down from the ridge top. We dashed to the next grove, and then the next, avoiding the taller trees. The rain was coming down in sheets.

Drenched, we half ran, half stumbled, to the large forested area near the bottom of the trail. We picked our way through the trees down to where we had parked our Honda. It was up to me to get the car in the open field that, with the unceasing thunder claps and lightning flashes, resembled a World War I battle scene.

Thinking how cruel it would be to get scorched by lightning this close to safety, I took a deep breath and dashed across the clearing, sprinting fifty yards in 4.8 seconds. I unlocked the car door and threw myself inside.

That evening back at the cabin, we munched on hamburgers and fries from the local grill, me clenching that cherished beer. Although too exhausted to say much, I think we all felt more durable, tougher, after the day's experiences. I did have to admit that my plan for the outing might have benefited from a little more fine tuning. This idea of wilderness demands respect. Our most important discovery this day was, in going to the Mokelumne Wilderness, we had gone to more than just a place.

Travels With Kirk

Our first trip to the Mokelumne Wilderness produced one irreversible outcome—the canyon had seized my oldest son's heart and soul. From that day forward, maybe inspired by the fish he lost, or by other unknowns, Kirk's first choice for a camping and fishing destination was the Mokelumne Wilderness. He usually persuaded me to join him.

We never took a one-day trip again, instead packing in for at least one or two nights. After completing the grueling hike out with a heavy backpack, I swore more than once never to do it again. But Kirk's persistence and the Mokelumne's allure proved irresistible time after time.

The October following that first trek, the boys and I planned another trip there. Fashioning a hiking staff from an oak sapling, I figured I'd be prepared for any wayward reptile. A mounted rattlesnake skin, like one I saw displayed in a local tavern, would make a nice addition to our cabin, I thought—a symbol of our wilderness bravado.

After reaching the river and setting up camp, I poked my staff in and around rocks and fallen logs looking for a rattler. The following morning I did the same. No luck. Any snakes in the vicinity were not about to expose themselves and get clubbed.

That afternoon the boys and I fished downriver. On the way back to our camp, I was in the lead, my mind still absorbed by the river's currents and their trout.

Walking right behind me, Doug suddenly exclaimed, "Dad, don't move."

Right. With the reaction of a frog hitting hot water, I executed a triple jump that would have won at most track meets. When I looked back at my launching pad, I saw a three-foot rattler extended on the sandy clearing, motionless, attempting to go unnoticed. This open spot was the last place I expected to see a rattler. Yes, being the tough outdoorsman I was, I killed the defenseless creature, carting its skin to the cabin to display on the wall.

On occasion, Kirk persuaded a friend or two to join him on forays to the Mokelumne. One lucky companion, Randy, picked up a twenty-two-inch brown. He was so proud of his catch that he lugged it out in his backpack the hot afternoon of the next day. By the time he and Kirk arrived at our cabin, the trout's rotting flesh meant Randy could only display his prize to the assemblage from a considerable distance.

Kirk sold his Mokelumne tales to another buddy, Mark, who had never fished before. For the trip Mark purchased a complete fishing ensemble: rod, reel, line, leader, flies. Kirk forged a new trail straight down the almost impenetrable canyon side, not knowing Mark had bad knees. By the time they reached the canyon floor, Mark's knees ached so severely he had to rest them for two solid days before he could hike out. Never did he wet his line.

A favorite trip etched in my memory occurred when Kirk and I hiked a loop. We camped the first night of this eighteen-mile trip at Camp Irene. After lashing our backpacks to a makeshift log raft, we crossed the river the next morning, and then hiked down the canyon to Cedar Camp. The primitive trail, sculpted out of stone in places and barely discernible in parts, had been the work of the Civilian Conservation Corps during the '30's.

Cedar Camp, sitting within massive old growth cedars and pines, was little disturbed by man's intrusions. Numerous Indian grinding holes carved in nearby granite revealed earlier visitors. It was easy to imagine Native Americans spending their summers in this rich setting, grinding acorns, hunting, catching salmon and trout. After a night's stay, Kirk and I hiked to Grouse Valley, recrossing the river on a large fallen tree trunk. Another night of camping riverside, and then it was back to Highway 4 up the mountainside via the Grouse Valley trail to complete the loop.

Many black bears call the Mokelumne Wilderness home, although I've never encountered one. I have seen plenty of bear sign, including a huge pile of berry-filled scat on a flat rock in the middle of the river, allowing me to conjure up quite a memorable river scene.

It's easy to imagine this wilderness also being home to the venerable grizzly bear, *ursus arctos californicus*, as surely it was. California's designated state mammal, this magnificent creature once numbered 10,000 in the Golden State. The grizzly systematically was eliminated throughout most of the western states, with the last central Sierra specimen taken in 1895. The last California grizzly bear was killed in Sequoia National Forest in 1922.

When one hikes the Mokelumne Wilderness, the size of the trees strikes the eye. Here stand the giants of the pine family—the Ponderosa or Yellow Pine, and the Sugar Pine which John Muir called "the noblest pine" in the world. The Sugar Pine, a personal favorite, was named for the sweet gum that exudes from wounds in the trunk, rivaling maple sugar in sweetness. It is the tallest and largest of the world's pine trees, capable of reaching heights of 200 feet and diameters exceeding nine feet. With a unique asymmetrical, scraggly shape, the Sugar Pine's longest limbs are near its top, and from them hang giant cones, often over twenty inches long, the world's largest. The bottom third of the tree is without limbs.

Unfortunately these giants have been so reduced throughout the West by man and by white-pine blister rust that old growth specimens are few across the Sierra. In fact, eighty five percent of the Sierra's ancient pine and fir forests have been logged, with Sugar Pines the first to be heavily decimated in the mid-Nineteenth Century.

When I looked at these old specimens, several centuries in age, I realized they bore witness to the comings and going of the Indians, mountain men, and the wild animals that roamed the area. I felt a sense of history, and melancholy, like paying homage to past war heroes. Standing among these majestic

21

trees, one can see and take in sufficient evidence of their irreplaceable value.

The hike out of the Mokelumne Wilderness with a backpack is a killer, even without bears, rattlesnakes and lightning. Surely one emerges from this untrammeled area a different person, with a greater awareness of the beauty and challenges of wilderness. Forest Ranger Bob Wetzel referred to the Mokelumne Wilderness as a "magical but daunting place." I can understand Kirk's attachment to it. I share it with him.

Monte Wolf: A Frontier Spirit

A presence one may sense in the Mokelumne Wilderness is that of the last person to have lived here, Monte Wolf, a veritable Twentieth Century mountain man. Wolf changed his real name, Ed McGrath, to conform with his Indian mother's background. After World War I he lived in a series of makeshift camps throughout the central Sierra. In the early 1930's, he came to the Mokelumne canyon where he built a five-room log cabin in the canyon's upper reaches, and a second cabin lower down, both entirely of native materials.

At 5'7" and 160 pounds, Wolf was not a big man, but he was strong and dogged. Reportedly he hauled an iron wood-burning stove on his back for fourteen miles. He also lugged a keg of nails weighing over a hundred pounds to his cabin from an abandoned work site at Salt Springs Reservoir.

Many legends exist about this mysterious hermit with long black hair. He was reputed to be a thief but people who knew him swore otherwise. Some people feared him. On one occasion he and another man, a professional fighter, simultaneously showed up at a cabin far back in the mountains of Tuolumne County. The owner had given both men permission to use the cabin, not expecting them to show up at the same time. In a scene reminiscent of the early frontier, the two men argued, and then fought for thirty minutes with Wolf not giving an inch. When Wolf seized an ax, the second man, fearing for his life, grabbed a nearby steel crowbar, ending the fight in a standoff.

Wolf trapped coyote, mink, otter, martin and bobcat during the long winters. He established "spike camps" throughout the Sierra stocked with food and supplies to make his forays easier. He would also drop in unexpectedly on acquaintances, spending an hour or a night. Sometimes he would depart in the middle of the night, lending credence to his reputation as a strange person. In the winter, he strapped skis to his feet to tramp through Sierra blizzards and heavy snow that might have taken the lives of less hardy individuals. During summers, he would guide interested visitors in fishing the Mokelumne's waters.

If someone asked me in the mid '70's what I thought of Monte Wolf, my answer would have been shallow and undeveloped. Like many Americans, I am fascinated with mountain men and the early frontier. The frontier spirit has been one of the most dominant strains in the American character. Monte Wolf was unquestionably a throwback to the days when trappers and Native Americans roamed the vast west, living off the land and killing for food. But with the closing of the frontier in the 1890's, how acceptable was it for someone to continue living the life of a mountain man on public lands well into the Twentieth Century?

In truth, back in the 1960's and 1970's when I was emerging from an academic cocoon, I never seriously thought about such matters. My generation inhaled second-hand cigarette smoke without question. Our parents wore fur coats. I spent my childhood near rivers that daily received deadly chemical discharges from factories, killing every living thing in and around the water. I breathed air polluted by smokestacks. I grew up accepting such practices as the way things are. So in 1975, I didn't think or question whether, in the Twentieth Century, any individual should be able to live in a wilderness, cut trees to build cabins, kill animals without restrictions.

Monte Wolf disappeared one spring in the early 1940's never to be heard from again. A fishing pole found on a rock along the Mokelumne's bank suggested he drowned. The ambitious hiker can visit both of his cabin sites. The Forest Service set his upper cabin ablaze in the late 1970's due to the amount of trash people were leaving there, it being only a few miles from the highway. The Forest Service is not entirely happy with the efforts of Monte Wolf's friends to maintain the lower cabin as a usable manmade structure deep in a designated wilderness area.

Today a skier can carve turns down the "Monte Wolf" run at the Bear Valley Ski Resort and gaze, as I have done numerous times, into the canyon far below where this rugged individual relived early frontier days, where Native Americans enjoyed their summer paradise, where grizzlies roamed freely, where trout and salmon thrived in emerald waters of a magnificent river, and where stands of old growth trees continue to supply the nutrients of life.

2
Becoming A Fly Fisherman: New Zealand

New Zealand is the fly fisherman's Shangri-la.—**Zane Grey**

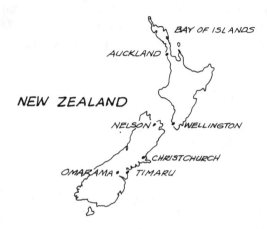

The first people to inhabit New Zealand were the Maoris, believing the country's two islands were created when Kupe, a man-god, cut a giant fish abandoned by another man-god, Maui. Today, the Maoris comprise only thirteen percent of New Zealand's population, yet their culture remains forever embedded in the names of the country's rivers, towns and sites.

New Zealand is located midway between the Equator and South Pole, with a range of latitudes similar to California, although in opposite halves of the globe. The country, whose heritage is predominantly English, is similar in size to Japan, Britain or Italy. Australia lies approximately 1000 miles to the west, separated from New Zealand by the Tasman Sea.

The presence of volcanic mountains and thermal regions in the North Island, spectacular mountain ranges and fiords in the South Island, magnificent sea coasts outlining the entire country, and innumerable lakes and swift rivers everywhere, make New Zealand a land of unparalleled natural beauty. The sportsman has a wide array of outdoor adventures to choose from, including unsurpassed fly fishing.

25

Trout are not native to New Zealand's waters. The country imported the two predominant fresh water species—brown and rainbow trout—in the second half of the Nineteenth Century. The brown trout ova came from England in 1868, and the rainbow trout from California's Sonoma Creek in 1983 (a sea-run steelhead fish). These species have adapted so successfully that New Zealand's trout fishing is considered among the world's best.

Settling In

New Zealand was the first and only destination to intrigue me enough to plan an extended international vacation. I possessed a clear motive—fly fishing for big trout. While Diane was as excited as I about the thought of spending as much as a year in this faraway land, our teenage kids were not as convinced of its merits. Daughter Jennifer quickly opted out altogether, deciding instead to try Utah's ski slopes on the way to becoming a ski instructor. Sons Kirk and Doug, although reluctant to leave school and friends behind for such a length of time, eventually came around.

Now all we needed was to work out the logistics. Fortunately, a high school in my district was closing, presenting me with a unique opportunity to take an extended leave. Diane's position at the hospital also allowed for a prolonged absence.

Although we had initially planned to go for a full year, my boss had second thoughts about me being gone for so long. With the boys pushing for a shorter trip, we finally settled on three months. We would leave late October and return in January, taking advantage of New Zealand's summer months.

The boys would carry out their studies through independent study, arranged in advance with their teachers.

After studying maps and books on the country, we tentatively selected the small town of Timaru on the South Island as home base. Located approximately 100 miles south of Christchurch, Timaru was described as a popular coastal town with mild climate, good swimming, and lots of nearby trout streams.

Our trip would begin in Auckland. We would tour the North Island before ferrying across Cook's Strait to the South Island. Other than the first night's lodging, and a trek on the famous Milford Track, we made no other prior arrangements.

On October 27, our Pam Am jet lifted off the San Francisco runway, and some fourteen hours and 8000 miles later, landed in Auckland. The New Zealand Immigration officials delayed our entry by requiring us to open all of our bags and trunks ("don't have any dried mud on your hiking boots, do you mate?"). The bus driver and his Kiwi passengers waited for us with patience and good cheer.

After checking into our motel, Diane and I went for a walk to explore the surroundings. For our first New Zealand dinner that evening, we stopped at a local market and bought lamp chops, a much anticipated fare. When we returned to the motel at 5 p.m., Kirk announced he was going jogging, saying he would be back in an hour.

When he hadn't returned by six thirty, I was perturbed. When he wasn't back by seven, I was downright angry. At seven thirty, I was concerned. By eight, I was frantically worried that he was lost, or worse. I called the police to report a missing person. The officer's response (I later learned that New Zealanders are low key about most things) was not to worry, that "he'll turn up."

Kirk returned to the motel at eight thirty, out of breath and embarrassed. He got his streets mixed up, and only knew our motel as a "Best Western." We ate our lamb chops late that night.

Rex's Auto in Auckland supplied us with a "guaranteed buy back" vehicle, a two-door Toyota station wagon registering over 95,000 miles. We secured non-deductible insurance at a reasonable rate—a fortuitous arrangement as later events would tell. Strapping our two huge chests atop the roof, and squeezing the rest of our stuff in the wagon, we departed Auckland, avoiding several near collisions as I adjusted to driving on the left side of the road, with the steering column, shift and pedals on the wrong side of the car.

After motoring north of Auckland to spend a few days at the beautiful Bay of Islands, we made an ill-advised trip to the west coast to see the giant Kauri tree—New Zealand's equivalent to California's Redwood. We could barely see the trees through a drenching downpour. After a quick look, we headed south on the island's major west coast highway—a narrow, dirt, now muddy, road.

Approaching Taupo 200 miles later, the Toyota began to heave and sputter. A ruddy mechanic told us a complete valve job was needed, taking a minimum of three days. I eventually calmed down, remembering Rex's Auto covered repairs. We intended to stop in Taupo anyway. But less than one week into our trip, our wagon had collapsed. Not a good omen.

Other than making a few casts, we didn't seriously fish the North Island, even in the renowned Taupo area, spending the majority of time sightseeing. When I fish, I don't want distractions; besides, I have seldomly caught fish in unfamiliar waters while traveling from one place to another.

Toyota repaired, we completed our tour of the North Island, ferried across Cook's Strait, and then drove the beautiful Queen Charlotte Drive to Nelson. After a quick stop in this handsome city, we pointed the car south toward Timaru, now anxious to see our chosen "hometown."

We found the Canterbury Plains south of Christchurch unimpressive, and the small towns near Timaru drab and uninteresting, causing us to wonder about our choice of locations. Timaru, however, proved different. We were pleased to find a large city park area with acres of grass, tennis courts, outdoor swimming pool, cricket fields, amphitheater, and picnic facilities, bordering lovely Caroline Bay. To fill out the picture all we needed was a house to live in.

The local newspaper showed no advertised home rentals, and our verbal inquiries were just as discouraging. After a desperate jaunt to an outlying town to check for rentals there, we returned to Timaru and ran our own ad: "American family of four wishes to rent house through January." Several responses came in, and we selected a handsome, two story, brick house two blocks from Caroline Bay for fifty dollars a week, utilities included.

Now we were ready to catch those trophy fish.

Kiwi Trout

Back in the states, the boys and I had done very little fly fishing, Kirk showing the most interest. I never felt confident with flies. But with New Zealand's reputation, we were resolved to abandon bait fishing and become fly fishermen.

Why fly fishing? There were the usual reasons. When one bait fished, handling slimy nightcrawlers stored in dirt produced dirty hands and fingernails. And when one retrieved swallowed bait hooks from a trout's gullet, one usually wound up with cut fingers and hands. Then there were the containers of smelly, rotten worms inevitably left in the fridge, and later discovered by one's wife.

By comparison, fly fishermen generally wore nicer clothes, looked and acted neater, and seemed more sporting than bait fishermen. Most important, however, was that mystique about fooling a fish with an artificial fly. We were ready to discover what it was all about.

Although fishing guides are available to help a newcomer catch fish, I have never hired one and had no inclination to start, being independent-minded as well as cheap. To me, fishing involves gathering information and learning how to do it on your own. Besides, given New Zealand's reputation, I thought why waste money in a can't miss situation?

We checked with a local sports shop owner who directed us to a number of the area's prime streams. He spoke of average catches in the one- to three-pound range, with five pounders possible, and mentioned night fishing as a good bet. My brain ignored this notion, the mechanics of fishing being tough enough when I can see.

The next day, the boys and I left to try our luck on the Hae Hae Te Moana stream outside nearby Temuka. We expected the late afternoon and early evening hours to provide prime fishing just like the Sierra waters we were used to.

The small stream disappointed us, causing us to wonder how large trout could survive in it. Unlike our favorite California rivers that crashed down steep gradients, the flat Hae-Hae-Te-Moana slowly meandered through a heavily willowed and grassy shoreline.

Feeling as though we were on a different planet, we started casting our flies, half expecting immediate strikes from the likes of fish the store owner had cited. No such luck. We didn't glimpse any trout in the open water, and it was impossible to get a fly under the overhanging willows where fish, if there were any, might be holding. Four hours later, we gave up without so much as a single greeting from a trout.

For days we repeated this pattern, with the days becoming weeks. Changing rivers made no difference. They were all the same—flat. The few trout we managed to spot, including several big ones, quickly glided back under willows. As the number of unsuccessful outings kept mounting, our frustration and discouragement compounded.

Through persistence, we did manage to hook an occasional fish. My first catch was a fat, fifteen incher that savagely hit my spinner (I had resorted to using spinning lures), in a pool on the Pareora River, known as one of South Canterbury's best rivers before local farmers diverted most of its water for irrigation. At first I didn't recognize the trout species, it being silvery in color with no clear markings. We later learned that sea-run browns in these coastal streams possess this silvery hue.

Another day, while enjoying a picnic near a small pond, we noted dimples on the surface. Fly rod in hand, I cast a nymph pattern (a fly fished underwater to simulate an immature aquatic insect) to a promising swirl. On my second cast, I felt a strong resistance, followed by line being ripped from my reel. A hefty fish streaked toward the center of the pond, leaped high from the water, and then contested and tugged at the hook impaled in its mouth. Minutes later, I brought in my first New Zealand trout caught on a fly—a seventeen-inch rainbow—inspiring me to think that perhaps this fly fishing wasn't so difficult after all.

Later, on the Clinton River along the Milford Track, a six-pounder approached Kirk's fly, causing his heart to skip a few beats. Too savvy, the fish swerved away at the last second. Kirk caught his maiden fish—a brightly colored, fourteen-inch rainbow—on a dry fly in a small stream in Omarama, causing his confidence to jump several notches.

Doug's experiences were bedeviling. In the Te Anau area where the Milford Track begins, he drifted a spinning lure in a section of stream under a bridge. A large trout shot from the shadows and savagely struck his lure. Hook in mouth, it raced downstream. When Doug attempted to muscle it back against the strong current, the big brown wrenched itself free. Another time, a monster trout tore into his fly on a waterway connecting two lakes, but it also sped off, broken leader and fly in mouth.

Doug landed his first trout, a thirteen-inch brown that struck his spinner on the Hai-Hai-Te-Moana. Not a big fish, not caught on a fly, but after five weeks, it was a catch.

So after spending countless hours fishing the richest trout fishery in the world, all we could manage was an occasional hookup. Getting New Zealand trout to hit flies seemed near impossible. Determined to catch fish at all costs, I weakened and dug up some nightcrawlers.

The next time out, I spotted a good-sized fish glide back under a rock. I drifted a weighted fly past the trout's lie several times, unsuccessfully. The trout left me with no choice but to turn to my old bait fishing skills. I placed a big, fat nightcrawler on a hook and let the current carry it down to where the fish was holding under the rock. I felt a slight tug. After giving the trout time to swallow the bait, I pulled back and brought a nice fifteen-inch brown to my net. Admittedly a serious regression in fishing tactics, I was now desperate enough to take a trout any way I could. Unfortunately this catch did not signal a change in luck. In fact, it would worsen.

Early one misty morning, Kirk, Doug and I left for fishing, hopes still running high. *Maybe today will be our breakthrough day*, I thought while speeding away from Timaru. Kirk wanted to fish the Opihi while Doug and I were going to try the nearby Temuka.

After a ninety-degree turn onto a dirt road leading to the Opihi, I dropped Kirk off. I then turned the Toyota around and with wheels spinning sped back out. Where the dirt road ended, forgetting I was in New Zealand, I glanced to my left instead of my right as I pulled out onto the paved country road.

"Dad, look out!" Doug screamed. All I recall was a large blur heading at us, screeching brakes and skidding tires, and a severe jolt accompanied by metal crushing and glass smashing. A farmer in a truck coming over a slight hill couldn't stop in time on the wet pavement to avoid hitting us. Fortunately he swerved just enough to spare us a direct hit.

The left front fender of the Toyota looked like a collapsed accordion. The farmer's truck looked worse. A tow truck hauled my vehicle to the "panelbeaters" for a three-week stay, causing me to be grateful for the cheap insurance I secured, although the cost of a rental car hurt. True to character, the farmer apologized for his part in ruining our day of fishing.

At this point, our once-in-a-lifetime trip had not provided a once-in-a-lifetime fishing experience. And we hadn't even hit bottom yet.

Barry's Way

Throughout our stay, we traveled frequently to other South Island locations. In the Mackenzie Basin area, when inquiring

32

about fishing prospects, someone told me of a fellow named Barry Thornton, a resident fisherman in Twizel. I called him and he invited us to his home.

Barry lived in a low-cost housing unit surrounded by tens of similar structures. More swarthy than the typical New Zealander, he said he was born and raised in Tasmania, an island off the Australian coast. With two young children running about the house, I figured him to be somewhere in his mid-to-late-thirties.

While chatting in his living room, I told Barry of our fishing woes. With a gleam in his eye, he offered to show us some of his techniques. I jumped at his offer. (I later learned Barry was a fishing guide, and was anxious to get the word out on his services.) We made plans to meet the next day in Omarama where my family was camping in a motor park.

Barry picked Kirk, Doug and me up in a beat-up station wagon and took us down a dirt road to the Ahuriri River. Dressed in shabby pants, tattered shirt, barnyard boots and a weathered cap sporting a number of beat-up flies, Barry did not inspire our confidence. He assembled his rod, pulled his leader through a piece of inner tube to "get the kinks out," coated his leader with mud from a pouch, slung a strap attached to a burlap bag over his shoulder, then said, "Let's go."

Barry took us to backwaters—overflow pools that form alongside a river's main channel. He hoped to spot big browns that cruise these backwaters in search of food. He said that if he could see a fish, he usually could "nail it."

To me, trout in slow, clear pools cannot be caught. Whenever I cast anything in this type of water, even bait, the fish immediately dart for cover. So when Barry stationed us on the bank overlooking one of these backwaters, I was more than a little skeptical.

The four of us sat and peered at the water. It was only three to four feet deep, clear as gin, with algae and aquatic grasses visible along the bottom. After ten minutes, a large brown trout came swimming our way. When it got close, Barry scrambled down the bank, making little effort to hide from the fish. He quickly made two short false casts, and then propelled the nymph at the end of his mud-coated leader directly at the fish, the fly piercing the water like a bullet. The fish struck instantly and Barry set the hook, with the boys and me watching in amazement.

"Good as gold, mate," Barry said as he passed me the rod so I could play the fish. After a couple of minutes I gave it back to him. He maneuvered the trout in close and, with a cotton glove on his left hand, grabbed the fish near its tail and hoisted the twenty incher from the water, dropping it in his burlap bag.

We resumed our positions on the bank. Before long another fish came cruising to our part of the pool. Barry repeated his demonstration. A charge down the bank, two quick false casts, a final swift cast that shot the nymph into the water directly in front of the fish; followed by a strike and setting of the hook. The boys took turns playing this second large brown before Barry said, "Good on ya, boys," and took the rod back.

We left that part of the pool. Barry and Doug walked to the narrow outlet channel while Kirk and I ambled over to the other side of the pool, where we waited behind a tree.

Pretty soon a big brown came swimming near where Kirk and I were standing. Still hidden behind the tree, I let out a short amount of line and then made a soft cast so the nymph dropped gently in front of the cruising brown. When the fly touched the water, the fish immediately bolted toward the exit channel, accompanied by my loud blaspheme.

I yelled to Barry that there was a fish coming his way. He got his rod ready, and when the streaking brown got close he made his short, thrusting cast. I'll be dammed if he didn't get that fish to strike his nymph. Only this time, Barry didn't hook it securely and the fish flopped off, causing him to mumble about the hook not being sharp enough. But he had gotten a fleeing brown trout to strike his fly!

Doug and Barry moved on to other backwaters. They spotted three more big browns, each of which Barry hooked. Kirk and I went fishless on the main river.

Since that day, I've pondered over Barry's technique many times, concluding there is one simple answer to his success. It's how he cast his nymph—short and hard as though his rod was a slingshot, placing the fly directly in front of the trout's nose, causing the fish to react quickly and instinctively. He didn't give the trout time to make a decision, it just reacted to a morsel of food suddenly before its mouth.

Barry took clients to nearby Benbow Lake where the Ahuriri flows, and stalked fish cruising the shallows, using polarized glasses to reduce the water's glare. Stalking big trout in the clear pools of rivers and streams, and along the shores of lakes, represents the "New Zealand way" of fly fishing. Barry's method, however, did not involve the standard techniques. He didn't try to hide from the trout, he made no attempt at a "natural" presentation, and the fly pattern meant little. Rather, he preyed upon a trout's instinctive behavior by thrusting his fly abruptly before the fish's mouth.

That afternoon along the beautiful Ahuriri River, Barry Thornton treated us to a rare exhibition of fishing genius. A master at getting big browns to strike his fly, Barry and his unconventional technique had to be seen to be believed.

Into the Night

During our New Zealand stay, we did more than just fish. We traveled widely, hiked extensively, took a thrilling jet boat ride in a narrow river gorge, swam, played tennis, and socialized with many New Zealanders whom we still count as friends. When the boys and I fished, Diane kept herself occupied with her own exploring.

Fly fishing was the one activity proving to be a bust. At the halfway point of our stay, we had caught a grand total of eight fish, only four on a fly. Only six weeks remained for us to turn things around.

One December morning, Diane took a train to Christchurch for a two-day excursion, leaving the boys and I uninterrupted time to fish. The first afternoon we headed to the challenging Opihi a mile upriver from its confluence with the Temuka. While Doug remained at the Opihi, Kirk and I cut overland and hit the Temuka.

In one run, Kirk and I spotted several nice browns holding near the bottom while a back current carried food to them. We tried repeatedly to interest them in our sunken nymphs, which they ignored. In another deep pool, Kirk sunk a nightcrawler on a rig he made with a stick, leaving it while we continued downstream. When he retrieved it later, at the end of the line was a writhing, five-foot eel. Kirk abruptly dropped the rig back into the water. Eels, some as long as six feet, populate most New Zealand waters, a disconcerting feature for those wading in shorts and sneakers as we did. Presumably eels can travel across land bridges to get to new waters.

True to form, Kirk and I lost track of time. Three hours had passed before we returned to the car. Doug was inside, tired and upset with our late return. He hadn't caught anything, although losing yet another good-sized fish. We drove to a café

36

in Temuka for dinner. That evening we would try the Hae Hae Te Moana. Silence hung over us as we ate, our morale and spirits at rock bottom.

Evening proved as frustrating as our day. With the sun setting, the boys packed it up and went to the car while I continued casting in the large pool near where we parked. After a few minutes Kirk yelled at me to quit. Just as I was about to, a fish jumped, followed by a second, and then a third. A trout, a big one, hit my fly. Surprised by the strike, I didn't set the hook.

It was now dark. The calls from the car were getting louder and angrier. I reluctantly reeled in my line, fixed upon returning tomorrow to fish at this time.

The next evening, feeding trout appeared just as the sun disappeared over the horizon. In total darkness, I cast my fly over and over into one pool, enjoying the most action I had experienced in six weeks. By midnight, I had caught seven browns in the ten- to fourteen-inch range, all on flies—a definite breakthrough. Driving back to quiet Timaru, I hummed a tune, knowing I had finally hit on something.

From that point on, the boys and I fished mainly at night. With over ten miles of fish-laden waters, the Temuka was our favorite river. We were soon catching as many trout in the ten- to fifteen-inch range as we could handle, and bigger ones most times out.

There was much to learn about fly fishing at night. All the problems that occur in daylight, e.g. line tangles, hang ups on branches, changing leaders and flies, tying knots, are exacerbated in darkness. We used a small flashlight (called a "torch" in New Zealand), usually held by our teeth, for our only light.

Fishing in the blackness of night sharpened our senses. We'd cast in the direction of a splash that we heard, feel the strike in our hands, and play the fish strictly through feel.

Trout would often feed just off of a bank, meaning we had to cast our fly close to the shoreline. Make it too long and we'd catch foliage and lose our fly. Our accuracy kept improving.

We checked out pools and tuned up our casting before darkness settled in.

We made ongoing adjustments. One time, Kirk was hooking trout after trout while I fished right next to him with no action at all. When I finally asked him what he was doing to produce strikes, he told me he pulled his fly across the water's surface, thus creating a small wake or disturbance which attracted the fish. A dead-drift float, the preferred strategy during daylight, proved less effective at night. Kirk had instinctively hit upon a productive tactic for fly fishing in the dark, one we used successfully from that point on.

The fly pattern seemed to make little difference to the fish, and I never learned what insects the trout were feeding on. We had good results with a Blue Dunn, March Brown, Royal Coachman, and a number of other patterns. A wet fly such as a Leadwing Coachman fished in the surface film also proved effective. Large-sized flies (#'s 10 to 12) proved more effective than smaller ones. The key though was what Barry and Kirk had demonstrated: It's what you did with the fly that counted most.

The maddening vagaries of the sport didn't vanish at night. For example, just before dark one evening, a number of nice trout began feeding aggressively in a stretch of ripples above a deep pool. For a solid thirty minutes I experienced great action in what seemed like a predictable feeding time and location for the trout.

Anxious for Doug to catch a trout above fifteen inches— our standard for a "countable" fish—I brought him to this stretch the next evening. Not a single fish was feeding in the ripples. The trout seemed to know when a newcomer arrived.

It wasn't until mid-January that Doug finally hooked his first countable, a fat seventeen incher. Technique down, he continued to bring in fifteen-plus inchers from that point forward. His best catch was an eighteen incher that fought savagely before going limp. When Doug brought it to shore, the brown had a deep gash near its head, the result of an apparent eel attack.

The number of trout over fifteen inches that we packed home kept growing. Kirk's best was a nineteen incher, the second best fish of the trip. Although these browns weren't the trophies New Zealand is noted for, we were more than satisfied by finally finding a river with an abundance of feisty trout that hit flies with abandon once the sun went down.

The Big One

With two weeks remaining in our stay, I returned to Omarama for two solid days of fishing while Diane and the boys drove to Mt. Aspiring National Park for some camping and hiking.

Since this was the Kiwis' summer, the motor park at Omarama was crowded. One camper, hearing me say that I haven't hooked any big fish yet in New Zealand, offered to take me eight miles outside of town to a good stretch of the Omarama. I gladly accepted.

The next morning, he deposited me by a wooden bridge, saying that big trout occupied the water here. The stream was only six to eight feet wide, but it ran deep in some spots. Near the bridge the stream flowed through a grassy field. Densely wooded areas encased the stream up and down from the field. A fierce wind that day made for difficult casting in the open meadow.

I walked slowly along the banks and caught glimpses of large shadowy forms retreating back under the bank and submerged tree roots. The current was flowing too swiftly, however, for me to place a nymph down to these spots. In the wooded section, I had no room for a backcast. As usual, it was tough New Zealand fishing.

Proceeding upstream, I approached a slow pool in a bend in the stream and saw a big trout feeding right on the surface. Transfixed, I stood behind a tree at the edge of the pool and observed the giant brown trout casually taking in whatever drifted to it. It must have been twenty-four inches, looking more like an alligator than a fish. If there was ever a golden opportunity for me to hook a lunker, this was it.

My main problem was getting a fly in the current without spooking the monster trout. A tree limb kept me from freely casting over the water. My only choice was to lower a fly down on a short line, maybe even spring it out like a sling shot.

Knowing that big browns like mice, I tied on a mouse pattern, figuring I could gently drop this heavier pattern into the current ahead of the fish. I carefully lowered the imitation rodent into the pool, and then let the current carry it down to the feeding fish. The flow took it slightly to the side and the fish moved over and inspected it. Not interested, the trout moved back to its feeding lane. Despite this failed strategy, the brown still showed no signs of apprehension.

I searched my fly box and selected a brown beetle pattern, one of the more popular New Zealand flies. With my rod positioned for a sideways cast under the tree limb, I shot the fly out onto the water. It and the line slapped the pool's surface, but the big brown wasn't rattled. As the beetle imitation drifted down current, the trout lifted its head and slurped it in.

When I pulled back to set the hook, I thought I could see the look of surprise in the fish's eyes. The rod bent under the heavy weight and the battle commenced. I chose to hold the fish securely in place, keeping a short rein. The fish pointed its head down, tugging strenuously back and forth. Soon I was up to my waist in water, holding rod with both hands, not giving the big brown any leeway.

Thinking I had to end this struggle by netting the fish, I attempted to raise it to the surface. When the trout saw the net, it fought fiercely, out of my control. By right I should have lost it, but somehow the hook held firm. The big brown again pointed its nose downward and tugged against the line while I held on.

Wondering about how I was ever going to land this bugger, I looked to the other side of the pool and saw a sandy beach. Inching my way across the pool, water up to my chest, I coaxed the tiring brown to follow me. When I got in shallow water, I pulled the big trout flopping onto the beach.

Back at the campground, the fellow who gave me the ride was almost as tickled with my success as I was.

Postscript

The day after I caught my big brown, the trout in the Omarama went on a hitting tear. I thought the key was my fly that resembled the horse flies all about the stream. But Doug, who had just returned late that afternoon with Diane and Kirk, also caught fish after fish, starting with a dry fly that soon lost all of its hackle. The trout continued to hit what now looked like a nymph. Soon he was fishing with only a hook with some remaining strands of thread, and still the trout struck. Although it lasted for just a couple of hours, we had finally experienced the kind of fly fishing we had come to New Zealand for.

By the end of our stay, we had caught thirty-eight fish, fifteen inches or better, plus triple that number of smaller ones, most taken from the Temuka. Not great, but for us, O.K. More important, we had made the transition to fly fishing, even though our modest success at it was helped by darkness, when inexperience and lack of finesse didn't matter.

At this time in our fishing careers, we kept all the fish we hooked except for small ones. Diane prepared them to eat in every conceivable way—frying, poaching, barbecuing, in salads, in stews, and in sandwiches. Before leaving, we gave trout to many of our Timaru friends.

Speaking of food, after that first lamp chop dinner in Auckland, we had several more lamp chop dinners, plus lamb hamburgers, lamb hot dogs, lamb sausage, lamb stew, rack of lamb, lamb kebobs, and lamb roasts. Every food we ate began to taste like lamb. Nothing hit the spot like an all-beef McBurger in Auckland our last day.

Leaving Timaru for the last time the Toyota now had 105,000 miles on it. It had lost all its power, chugging and laboring up every hill while we held our breath, praying it would get us back to Auckland. It did, but barely. We pulled into Rex's Auto, the Toyota sputtering and smoking. Rex turned white when I handed over the bills. He had clearly lost money on this guaranteed buy-back deal.

Happy about returning to the states, we were nevertheless sad to leave this fabulous country—its friendly, trusting people, its magnificent mountains and rivers, and the wonderful wild trout we had finally uncovered.

3
Making Connections: Small Streams

It is not the notion of the wilderness for its own sake that is of value, but the awareness of one's relatedness to it, one's utility with it, that deepens and extends the scope of human life.—**Ashley Montagu, Wilderness in a Changing World.**

The Mokelumne watershed lies between Highways 4 and 88. Three major forks—the North, Middle and South— plus numerous small steams, make up this extensive river system.

The North Fork, the largest waterway, flows from Highland Lakes at the 8,500-foot level to its eventual rendezvous with the Sacramento River in the Central Valley. After the Mokelumne Wilderness, the Salt Springs Reservoir interrupts the river's flow before it crashes through another rugged canyon, offering fourteen more miles of wild river. The Mokelumne is then tamed by a series of large reservoirs before joining the Sacramento.

The smaller, stream-fed Middle and South forks each flows for more than twelve miles through private lands mainly owned by Sierra Pacific Industries. The area is laced with dirt roads and has been extensively logged.

Except for a few specimens along the steep canyon banks, old growth trees have long since been removed.

The South Fork cuts through one of the deepest canyons in the Sierra, thus discouraging access and timber removal. A small piece of the Stanislaus National Forest—less than eight square miles—encases a lower stretch of this back country rivulet. Here, the Little Mokelumne joins the South Fork.

Back Roads

You've got to get up early if you want to catch fish. That's the rule I used to follow, a residue more from my early New England training than from fishing results. Groaning when I switched on the cabin lights at 5:00 a.m., the kids would roll out of bed, dress, and eat their cold cereal in silence. Then it was out into the darkness, and a bone-rattling jaunt on old logging roads to our stream of choice, usually arriving at daybreak.

Our favorite waters were the Mokelumne's Middle and South forks. Reaching one of these isolated rivulets, we'd put on our "creek shoes," and bushwhack our way through brush, climb over rocks, and slosh through the stream to reach stretches that seldomly saw other anglers.

Most times the catch didn't justify our efforts, if fish were indeed our sole objective. What fueled our spirits was the hope we would locate a hidden sanctuary holding numerous wild trout, including one or two larger than our typical eight-to-ten-inch catches.

After a half day of fishing, I would round up my companions, not always easy in these rugged surroundings. If we had separated without specifying meeting time and place, I would have to guess whether they were upstream or downstream. Did I leapfrog over them, or they me? Head the wrong direction and I would expend many minutes calling out and trampling the stream banks until I found them, or they me. Then, hot, tired and dirty, and feeling akin to the early mountain men who likewise pursued wild creatures, we trekked back to the car for the dusty drive home. After cleaning the trout, ourselves and most times the car, we would spend the rest of the day relaxing, playing tennis, swimming— a schedule describing many of our summer days.

Always searching for better fishing, we scanned maps to locate new access routes to those tantalizing blue lines indicating a stream. One day while pouring over a map, I noted a dirt road alongside the Little Mokelumne, a tributary of the South Fork. At the end of the road, the map showed a trail leading to the South Fork. The more I looked at this remote spot where the two streams joined, the more I wanted to go there.

A warm July day, I recruited Jen, Kirk and Doug to join me on an expedition to find the trail. We piled into our 1969 Plymouth station wagon, a well-traveled backroads vehicle sporting over 130,000 miles, and motored off.

From the town of Arnold, we took a gravel road to a summit, and then a dirt road down the other side. Where we crossed the Little Mokelumne, I turned the Plymouth onto a narrow road, if you could call it that, paralleling the stream. Judging from the overgrown brush scraping our wagon, it was obvious few cars traveled here. In a half mile we arrived at a crossing—a collapsed log bridge.

Exiting the car and surveying the scene, we spotted an even more obscure road leading off through tall grass. Not to be deterred, the troops and I got back into the wagon and pushed onward. A quarter of a mile later, we lurched over a dirt mound, the Plymouth coming to a halt in a depression. Ahead loomed a granite precipice.

We vacated the wagon, scooted to the top of a rocky incline, and scanned the countryside. We saw no sign of any trail. Off to our left the Little Mokelumne plummeted down a narrow gorge. Somewhere in front of us in blessedly untamed terrain, the South Fork flowed. Kirk insisted we could manage a way down, but I reluctantly decided that today was not the day.

When I attempted to back the Plymouth up, the tires spun in the dirt and the motor stalled. I fired it up and, with wheels churning, the old car lunged back and over the dirt mound, and stalled. I hit the ignition, but the engine only whirred. Several more attempts produced more of the same. Hoping the problem was only a flooded engine, and not one requiring a walk to town, I rested the motor for several long minutes. On my next effort, the Plymouth whirred, coughed and sputtered, then started. After getting it pointed in the right direction, not an easy feat, I drove back to Arnold knowing Kirk was right—we would find a way down to the South Fork the next time.

The following summer, Kirk and I planned our return to find that elusive trail. On this July day, we climbed into our canary-yellow 1974 Honda CVCC—a great little mountain car pushing 90,000 miles. Following the same route of a year ago, we reached the end of the dirt road where it overlooked the canyon. With daypacks on, fishing rods in hand, Kirk and I set out to locate the trail, or else blaze one.

Perched on a rock outcropping, we studied the terrain. To our left where the Little Mokelumne crashed down the gorge, we spotted a chute between two granite walls. We clambered over the rocky ridge to this entry point to the ravine and scrambled down the fifty-foot chute. We then slid down the remainder of the steep hillside to the base of a thundering waterfall. Now all we had to do was traverse down through the ravine.

We found sufficient room, first on one side of the stream, then on the other, to keep moving downstream, occasionally skirting beautiful deep pools encased by the rock walls of the gorge. After each platform of flat water, the stream plunges once again on its journey to the South Fork. Mosaics of ferns and mosses line the canyon sides, and an array of cascading water patterns and rock sculptures make this gorge a hidden wilderness gem.

We crashed through bushes and spider webs, and traversed rock ledges. It was an hour or so before we hit level ground. After another fifteen minutes of hiking through dense growth, we caught our first glimpse of the South Fork coursing through an alder-lined shoreline.

Kirk and I quickly set up our rods. From the stream's pools and rippled stretches, aggressive rainbows and an occasional brown seized our bait. In less than two hours we caught fifteen beautiful fish. We had located what we long sought—a remote section of stream brimming with wild trout.

We completed the hot hike out, our bodies sweaty and grimy, but our spirits high. At the car, we quenched our thirsts with cold drinks from our ice chest. Gear loaded, we were anxious to return to the cabin and a refreshing swim.

I started the Honda and backed up so I could turn it around on the narrow road. When I moved it forward, the front wheels went off the edge of the road and down an incline. When I tried to back up again, the front wheels (where the drive is located on a Honda CVCC) spun in pine needles and dirt, and the car slid further down the bank, where it stalled.

I set the emergency brake, fired the motor up again and hit the gas hard, spinning the tires furiously in the forest debris, the car sliding yet further down the hillside. This is not good, I thought. Any more slippage and we were in big trouble. I sat wondering what to do next.

I decided to give it one more shot. Hitting the ignition, I gave the Honda gas while simultaneously releasing the brake pedal, and in a gamble, rocked the car back and forth in what was now a dirt depression. On one backward heave, the wheels found solid ground and shot the vehicle up onto the road.

"Close call" I said to Kirk as he got in.

"Yeh, it would have been a long hike home," he replied with the slightest of chuckles.

Sobering Up

This stretch of the South Fork became a favorite destination, a place we returned year after year. With the poor roads and strenuous hiking discouraging other fishermen, we fished in exquisite solitude, always catching a bunch of wild trout. I saw evidence of other visitors only a couple of times, once finding a set of rusted car keys in the gorge making me wonder how the person had gotten home.

Throughout these years, I brought home all the fish caught. It never occurred to me not to. My wife loved trout for dinner, thus justifying my tardy returns. Plus it didn't seem as though I really caught a fish, especially a good-sized one, if I didn't show it to someone.

To pack out my catch, I carried an insulated container. I'd pop in a beer or soda packed with ice beforehand. After a hot and exerting hike, I'd drink up the cold beverage, and then fill the space with fish for the trek out.

On Doug's first excursion down the South Fork, he, Kirk and I loaded our backpacks to spend the night streamside. That evening, after a couple of hours of great fishing, we ate fire-roasted hot dogs, beans and sauerkraut. I retired that night in the flickering light of the campfire knowing this was as good as it will ever be.

The next day we made a discovery in the Little Mokelumne gorge. While ascending the narrow ravine, we fished the pools of the tumbling creek. In each, a good-sized brown, up to thirteen inches, seized our worms. We wondered how these beauties found their way to such an isolated section of creek. It was a good mess of trout we packed home that day.

Year after year, I fished these waters four or five times a season, seldomly disappointed. I eventually located a legitimate, although circuitous trail, traversing the mountainside. I often visualized this spot during the winter months. With the arrival of trout season, I anxiously packed up and returned to these enchanting streams, happily tramping through the rough wilderness, the freshness of spring in the air.

In the summer following our New Zealand trip, Kirk and I headed to the South Fork, eager to use our newly acquired fly fishing skills. We set out to fish far downstream.

From the confluence of the Little Mokelumne and South Fork, we forged our way along the dense stream bank. After a half mile, the South Fork dropped over a granite ledge out of our sights. Completing its fifty-foot drop, the stream flowed through a bowl-shaped chasm. We traversed the chasm's upper sides, making each footstep count.

Now streamside, we cast our flies into deep, green pools, catching several plump rainbows. We pushed further downstream. Below a small waterfall, I lowered a black, Wooly Worm fly into the churning whitewater, letting it get swept under the falls. Feeling a tug, I set the hook and pulled up a thick fourteen-inch rainbow, thrashing fiercely.

On our way back, we approached a long pool with the current swinging close to a bank in a bend. We spotted a good-sized trout holding on the surface in a classic feeding lane.

"Go ahead," I said to Kirk.

"Good as caught," he replied.

Kirk positioned himself and made a gentle cast, dropping his dry fly four feet upstream of the feeding fish. The current took the fly down and the trout engulfed it without hesitation. Kirk raised his rod, hooking the trout. It jumped high from the water, and streaked to the head of the pool. It then raced back toward where we stood. Straining against the hook, the trout shot downstream, and leaped again out of the water.

Kirk landed the spirited fish—a full-bodied brown, glistening with a golden-orange hue and dotted with jewel-like black and red spots. It was a wondrous example of a wild trout, outclassing any fish we had caught in New Zealand. This brown and my rainbow were the best a small Sierra stream offers. With the cleaned trout tucked away, we hiked up and out, not thinking of the serious flaw in this idyllic scenario.

My wake-up call didn't come until the next year. On a mid-summer's day, Kirk and I again departed for the South Fork. After completing the trek down the gorge, we pushed downstream, circumnavigating the chasm. We wanted to hit the prime pools where we had caught those fourteen-inch beauties the previous year.

Thousands of Lady Bird Beetles clustered along the shoreline greeted us. Known as *Hippidamia convergens*, or "convergent beetles," these beetles leave the lowlands at the beginning of summer, taking wind currents to the mountains where they breed along the streams and spend the ensuing nine months. In early spring, they emerge from winter hibernation, returning to the lowlands to feast on insects. Then it's back to the mountains to complete their yearly cycle.

We didn't hook a single fish that day, an unusual occurrence for the South Fork that I blamed on the beetles and low-water conditions in this drought year. We got skunked in the Little Mokelumne as well.

I returned the following spring and hooked only a couple of small rainbows in the South Fork, and nothing in the Little Mokelumne. I saw few signs of trout occupying these streams as in past years. Walking empty handed back to the car, I pondered the poor fishing long and hard. Usually my insulated container would be full after a day's fishing here. Awareness slowly began seeping into my brain, and I soon reached the obvious conclusion: I had played a key role in reducing the wild trout. One can't keep killing fish and expect the population to continue.

I thought of all the splendid fish we had carted home past summers. I recalled the fun the boys and I had upon first discovering the browns in the Little Mokelumne's spectacular gorge. With pain I thought of those fourteen-inch gems Kirk and I pulled out that one day, wondering how much bigger they might have grown.

With the absence of these trout, I realized the magnitude of my loss, and how I had contributed to weakening this wild place. From this point on, I resolved to return all wild trout caught.

Now when I hook a trout, I recall those times when such an incident meant one less, irreplaceable wild trout in two small mountain streams. To outsmart a trout with a fly still gives me tremendous enjoyment. But today, after looking at my catch, marveling its beauty, I release it gently and hurriedly back to its home.

4
A Matter Of Values: The Stanislaus

Every cañon commends itself for some particular pleasantness; this for pines, another for trout, one for pure bleak beauty of granite buttresses, one for its far-flung irised falls; and as I say, though some are easier going, leads each to the cloud shouldering citadel—**Mary Austin, The Land of Little Rain.**

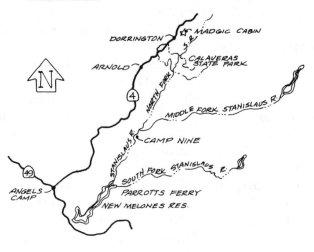

The Stanislaus River System is comprised of three major rivers: the North Fork, Middle Fork, and South Fork. The North Fork, largest of the three, begins high in the Sierra above Bear Valley and Lake Alpine, and flows through a rugged canyon on the south side of Highway 4. After 40 miles, it meets its sister forks in what was once the famous nine-mile Stanislaus rafting run, drowned when filled by the New Melones Reservoir in 1980.

The Middle and South forks start in the Emigrant Wilderness off Highway 108—the Sonora Pass Highway. The Middle Fork is quite accessible in its higher reaches, paralleling the highway for a number of miles. It then slices through a deep canyon extending many miles before joining the North Fork at Camp Nine.

Running through National Forest lands above and below the town of Strawberry along Highway 108, the South Fork is the least accessible of the three. It flows into the New Melones Reservoir.

With the names of many rivers and sites in the Sierras based on Indian, Spanish and Anglo origins, the Polish name "Stanislaus" seems unusual. The original Miwok name for the river was "Lakishumna," meaning "waters teeming with fish." These Native Americans lived along the Lakishumna, fishing for salmon, steelhead, and trout, and hunting antelope, deer and elk. They grew crops on the rich Stanislaus floodplain, and gathered acorns from the native oaks in the foothills to make acorn soup and bread.

Spanish explorers and soldiers were the first white men to explore the region, followed by missionaries who came to convert the natives. The priests established missions throughout California in order to house and educate the Indians, many of whom were brought unwillingly.

In rounding up rebellious natives, Mexican soldiers met fierce resistance from an Indian chief the missionaries called "Estanislao" in honor of the Polish saint, Stanislaus. This warrior fought so bravely and successfully in the river canyon against superior Mexican forces that the famed western explorer, John C. Fremont, used the chieftain's anglicized name in referring to the river.

The name stuck. Thus we have a river named by an Anglo-American in honor of an Indian chief named by Spanish missionaries to pay homage to a Polish saint. The Stanislaus is truly reflective of California's multicultural heritage.

The famed mountain man, Jedediah Smith, was the first American to explore the Stanislaus area after successfully crossing the Sierra in 1827 near the present-day Ebbetts Pass. In 1841, John Bidwell led the first emigrants over the Sierra before settling in the lower foothills. With John Marshall's discovery of gold in 1848 on the American River, hordes of gold seekers descended upon the region, degrading much of the landscape through their mining activities. Towns sprouted throughout the foothills. The richest mine in the central Sierra foothills was the Melones. Located on a hillside overlooking the Stanislaus, the Melones produced a 214-pound nugget—the largest piece of gold ever found in the United States.

Writer Bret Harte dubbed Melones "Roaring Camp," basing a book of short stories, *The Luck of Roaring Camp*, on his experiences. Mark Twain's short story, *The Celebrated Jumping Frog of Calaveras County*, which first brought him notoriety, was based on the famed frog contest held in nearby Angels Camp where it continues each year to this day.

Shooting The Staircase

The North Fork of the Stanislaus comprises a dominant thread in our family's tapestry. Running through a spectacular canyon below our cabin, it is the river we visited most.

We logged hundreds of hours of hiking and fishing along the dark, green waters of the Stanislaus. The river sports over forty miles of spectacular runs through a granite-sculpted gorge, huge boulders and verdant forests flanked alongside. The lower Stanislaus once flowed through the deepest limestone canyon on the west coast. From Camp Nine to Parrotts Ferry nine miles downriver, caves containing Indian petroglyphs and artifacts, miners' gear and other historical remnants, laced the canyon walls.

Whitewater enthusiasts discovered the Stan's rapids in the '60's. Within ten years this nine-mile stretch of river had grown into one of the country's most popular rafting runs. Scores of disabled persons—blind, deaf, crippled—came to the Stanislaus to experience the joys of its whitewater.

Always on the lookout for new family adventures, my wife booked a trip with a commercial rafting company, ARTA (American River Touring Association), in '74. Slamming into gushing holes, curlers and waves for the first time was both intimidating and invigorating. We crashed through the Stan's famous rapids: Cadillac Charley, Widow Maker, Death Rock, Devil's Staircase, Bailey Falls; we jumped off rock cliffs into deep, cold pools, picnicked in the shade of massive trees, and rested on sandy beaches.

Hooked on the sport, we were soon launching our own raft trips, using a yellow dinghy we called the "rubber ducky" to float down bouncy, tame stretches of river. And then I raised the bar several notches.

Midsummer in '75, Doug and I met two fellows who had just rafted the nine-mile stretch of the Stanislaus in a plastic, two-person boat. They described the run as "easy" due to low water. I looked at my nine-year old son who seldomly refused a challenge and said, "Let's do it." Unhesitatingly he agreed.

Diane brought the two of us to Camp Nine the next day, the mid-afternoon sun hot searing us with its heat. No other rafters were in sight as we inflated the dinghy, strapped on life preservers, and pushed off, wearing only tee shirts, shorts and sneakers.

When we reached a bridge a half mile downstream, we waved to Diane standing high above the river. She would pick us up at Parrotts Ferry, the end of the run. We bounced through the small rapid below the bridge, and as the current carried us further into the canyon, I looked back and saw Diane driving away.

Although the river was low as expected, the current was swift. And because the water came from the bottom releases of the upriver reservoir, its temperature was frigid. As the gradient dropped, the water picked up speed. A half mile from the bridge, the strong flow carried us over a cushion of water hiding a boulder. We slid sideways into the hole on the opposite side and the two of us toppled into the icy water. While holding onto the raft to keep it from going downriver, we climbed on a nearby rock. Jolted by the unexpected dunking, we got back into the raft and pushed off again, our confidence nicked.

Lacking ability to direct the dinghy, we rushed down the fast dropping river, the swirling, rushing current spinning us around, banging us off rocks like a pinball machine. Coming up fast, a tongue of swift water loomed, followed by an ominous looking wave that curled up and fell back upriver.

We raced down the tongue and hit the curler at a slight angle. The right front of the raft shot up in the air and arched back over our heads. Doug and I toppled into the frigid river. The strong current immediately clutched us in its icy grip, carrying us downriver, the overturned raft and paddles going on their own.

Shock gripped me. Not yet a quarter of the way into the trip, the stupidity of this venture was all too apparent. I looked back at Doug who was dog paddling, a concerned look on his face, but not panicking. Bobbing like corks, we were being swept toward another rapid, an ugly one.

The current carried me close to a rock shelf. I gripped a piece of ledge and pulled myself up onto the flat rock. As Doug fought the strong flow to get close, I grabbed his wrist and hoisted him up out of the water.

We sat there shivering, Doug's lips bluish. We pulled off our wet shirts and lay on the hot rock, letting the sun's rays warm us. Our raft and paddles were nowhere in sight. I lay there trying to think of what to do next, all options looking bad.

Downriver a person suddenly appeared, standing on a large rock, waving to us. We scrambled over boulders to reach him. Alongside his larger raft was our yellow dinghy and paddles that he and his crew had pulled from the river.

The fellow suggested we climb aboard their raft to run the next stretch that included Bailey Falls—a ten-foot drop. "You should be okay on your own after Bailey's," he offered.

The raftsman tethered the dinghy to his large Avon. After running Bailey's—a jolting drop even in the big raft—I felt the eyes of the other rafters as my young son and I climbed back into our flimsy craft, being more than a little embarrassed by my poor judgment this day. They pushed on ahead, Doug and I soon falling far behind, intent now only on completing the trip with no further incident.

When the sun dropped behind the canyon sides, our damp tee shirts kept us chilled. We paddled in silence, fearful of another dunking. But we encountered no more large rapids and managed to keep the dinghy upright the rest of the run. It was a welcome sight to see Diane waving to us from the Parrotts Ferry Bridge.

Doug and I often recall this ill-fated voyage and chuckle. Together we experienced some difficult moments that day and survived, creating even a stronger bond between us. It also increased our respect and appreciation for the power of whitewater, and for the Stanislaus.

A River Ran Through It

It wasn't long before I purchased a top-of-the-line whitewater raft. Now I was able to run the Stanislaus with renewed confidence, something I and a host of companions did often. Through trial and error, I eventually learned how to guide a raft in whitewater.

No singular gift of nature gave me, my family, and a widening circle of friends more fun and enjoyment than the turbulent, yet forgiving waters of the Stanislaus. Rafting brings people together like few other activities. Everybody pulls together to maneuver the boat through rapids, creating a team spirit. Other rafters provide encouragement and cooperation, leading to an unspoken bond among all river people, melded by the powers of the river itself. To sit on the banks of a river as beautiful and captivating as the Stan, lunching with comrades, replaying the day's excitement, is a singular nurturing experience not readily found elsewhere. And we kept returning to this river canyon, becoming ever more grateful for its gifts to us. Then it was taken away.

A massive dam had long been planned for the Stanislaus. First authorized in 1943, the dam received final approval nearly twenty years later. While we and others reveled in the river's currents, the Army Corps of Engineers was busy building huge bridges spanning the canyon. Unless halted, the New Melones Dam would create a mammoth reservoir twenty-four miles long, inundating the upper nine-mile canyon. But how does anyone halt the Army Corps of Engineers?

The Stanislaus River and its marvelous canyon were not well known outside of the small but growing cadre of whitewater rafters. Being a newcomer to the scene, I was befuddled about what was happening, outraged at the loss of a natural treasure, but resigned that powerful, governmental forces made such decisions. Along with most other river runners, I was a political novice. However, leaders emerged with strong ties to the Stanislaus such as Jerry Meral and David Kay who refused to accept its destruction.

In 1974, Meral and Kay mobilized river lovers and launched a frantic effort to stop the dam. Their strategy: gather the required 300,000 signatures to bring the issue of the dam to California voters as a ballot initiative. A loosely organized group calling itself "Friends of the River" (FOR) spearheaded the successful effort. I signed the petition, and tried to get as many of my friends and acquaintances to do the same, thinking the river might be saved after all.

The organizer of the pro-dam campaign, Milton Kramer, said, "It (the canyon) provides pleasure. We're so much in pursuit of pleasure that we're losing values that have built this country. It's the sign of a decadent society."

I agreed with Kramer on one point—it was a matter of values. At issue: a large reservoir fifteen miles in length that met all power and water storage needs identified for this project vs. a mammoth reservoir twenty-four miles in length that produced few if any additional benefits; the preservation of nine miles of a magnificent, one-of-a-kind river, and the deepest limestone canyon in the country vs. a standing body of water; the preservation of caves containing Native American petroglyphs and artifacts vs. a standing body of water; outdoor recreation for hundreds of thousands of people, including thousands of disabled persons, vs. another large lake available mainly to persons with motorboats (within a fifty-mile radius, this area of California contains seven large reservoirs).

In a crushing blow to river people, the dam forces won out when the initiative—Proposition 17—which would have placed the Stanislaus in the California Scenic Rivers System, failed. The pro-dam forces had cleverly couched their well-financed campaign as the one to "save the river," not clarifying it was the lower river in the valley the dam would "save." The strategy of deception worked as a post-election survey revealed that sixty percent of the people who voted intended to vote against the dam and for the wild river. But the disastrous result could not be reversed. Or could it?

The dam was completed in 1979, and the reservoir started to rise, bringing still water ever closer to Parrotts Ferry. In an act of desperation, Mark Dubois, a FOR leader, chained himself to a rock hidden along the river's edge to protest the filling of the canyon, while the water level rose ever closer to where he lay. His effort was publicized in the media, bringing increased national attention to the Stanislaus while symbolizing the resolve of river supporters. State and national leaders, including Governor Jerry Brown and President Jimmy Carter, supported the river's preservation. There was still hope.

Congressman Don Edwards introduced a bill to place the nine-mile stretch of the Stanislaus into the national wild and scenic system. The bill's passage depended on powerful Congressman Phillip Burton, a San Franciscan, a champion of the environment, and the Chairman of the House Steering Committee. If the bill passed—a good possibility—it would provide permanent protection for the Stan. With revived spirits, river supporters once again circulated petitions, sent letters, made phone calls.

The vote to bring the bill out of committee failed twenty to nineteen, shattering the morale of Stanislaus defenders yet again. Political realities ruled; river supporters, and more broadly environmentalists, did not yet have enough political clout to sway borderline politicians who responded primarily to vested interests. With the dam already built, leaving its grand design intact was the easier option to take.

Still FOR would not quit. The Antiquities Act allows the president, acting singly, to designate national monuments. In January, 1981, FOR went to President Jimmy Carter and requested he grant national monument status for the Stanislaus. Carter only had a few weeks left in office since Ronald Reagan had just defeated him in the 1980 election. Meanwhile, demonstrators once more assembled at Parrotts Ferry to rally support. Five members of the Stanislaus Wilderness Access Committee—a group of handicapped people and supporters—chained themselves to rocks just upriver of the rising water, having sent the key to their locks to President Carter. Unfortunately, the Iranian hostage crisis gave the president more than he could handle at this time, sealing the fate of the Stanislaus.

The New Melones Dam became the world's fourth largest earth-filled dam. Many of its supporters later conceded the presumed benefits of the dam— energy, flood control, water storage—could have been achieved with the smaller, less costly version that would have left the nine-mile canyon untouched, just as FOR had argued to no avail.

Every time I am at Camp Nine now, I cringe. The formerly vibrant, emerald green Stanislaus has been replaced by standing black water. When the reservoir is low, often the case, a huge bathtub ring, tree stumps and a lifeless riparian desert show where the rich, verdant canyon once exuded life. It was a matter of values all right. When I view this senseless transformation, a knot forms in my stomach, tears often coming to my eyes.

The only good results born from this irreplaceable loss were the birth of the Friends of the River organization, and the increased resolve of other environmental groups to preserve free-flowing rivers. In the struggle to save the Stanislaus, political amateurs had become political veterans. Building a dam in California, or anywhere, will never be that easy again.

Fishing the Untouched

Weaving through the mountains of the central Sierra, the three forks of the Stanislaus offer more than one hundred miles of good fishing. From readily accessible sections of rivers near roads and campgrounds, to remote stretches in deep canyons, the watershed provides many options.

A brochure from a new rafting company, Beyond Limits, prompted me to recall I had once heard of good fishing in the remote canyon sections of the Middle Fork. The flyer described a raft trip on a river "never before rafted," and a "pristine river canyon," complete with helicopter airlift to its put-in. Although the rafting sounded exciting, it was the image of fishing these waters that stuck in my mind.

Mike Lynch, one of the company's founders, answered the phone when I called. I asked him about the location of the canyon.

"It's not easy to describe," said Mike. "I'll put directions in the mail to you."

"How's the fishing there?" I asked.

"It can be good. You'll catch fish." he replied.

After receiving his directions, Kirk and I left on a November day to find the two-mile trail leading down to the river as shown on Mike's hand-drawn map. At Camp Nine we crossed the river and took a steep, torturous dirt road up the other side of the canyon. We then drove eight and a half miles on the worst rutted dirt road I had ever been on.

We stopped and spent an hour looking for the trail. No luck. Re-checking Mike's directions, I saw where we had missed a turnoff. We backtracked, found the turnoff, drove a half mile, and saw an obscure road leading down into the dense woods—the start of the trail. We got out of the car and started hiking.

For the first half mile, we walked on the old, twisting jeep road that turned eventually into a narrow path down the steep side of the canyon. With the mid-afternoon sun falling behind the mountain ridge, we walked quickly. We soon heard the roar of the river below. The last half mile was almost straight down, our toes pushing against the front of our hiking boots.

It wasn't until we reached the canyon floor that we got our first glimpse of the Middle Fork. The main channel here flows across a broad rock plateau before it and two side channels drop over a granite precipice in a triad of roaring waterfalls that crash into a big, dark blue pool. The river then flows in and around massive boulders on its plunging course down the rugged canyon.

Dense with growth, huge rocks everywhere, the shoreline presents a formidable course for the fisherman to travel. We had found what we were looking for—a tumbling river set within a rugged canyon guaranteed to discourage all but the most determined.

We assembled our rods and started casting in the pools and runs near us, hooking ten small trout within an hour. Although salivating to explore more, we didn't want to hike out in the dark. We reluctantly ended our fishing, intending to come back the first chance we got.

Walking steadily to beat the onset of darkness, I pushed the limits of my stamina. We succeeded in reaching the car in just under two hours with daylight to spare.

Ten days later—the last weekend of trout season—we returned. In a fast gait, we made it to the river in an hour and fifteen minutes, and then worked our way downriver. With the water level low, we rock jumped back and forth across the river whenever shoreline obstacles blocked our travel.

The sun disappeared by 2 p.m. due to the lateness of the season and the canyon's depths, leaving the water shaded. On wooly worm flies sunk into pockets of holding water, we hooked several nice rainbows. Not many or large, but overall a respectable showing.

Absorbed with the repetitive movement of the river, and the rhythms of fly casting, it's easy to lose one's self in a place like this. On this particular day, an unexpected visitor interrupted Kirk's immersion in his surroundings. Or was he the interloper?

Kirk had stopped fishing to change his fly. I was downriver a short distance. After tying on a new pattern, he made a few false casts, and then launched his fly out onto the water, almost hitting a large bear taking a drink from the other side of the pool twenty feet away. Kirk yelled to me but the river's roar drowned his voice to both me and the bear. When the brown-colored behemoth finally looked up, he stared at Kirk as though trying to figure out what this strange creature was doing standing there with a long stick. Neither budged for several long seconds. Then the large furry mass turned on its heels and with its powerful legs tore swiftly up the canyon hillside, dislodging rocks and debris.

Seeing a bear in this canyon was as likely as seeing another human. In subsequent visits, we have seen much more bear spoor, e.g. huge berry-filled scat, than human spoor, e.g. beer and soda cans, candy wrappers. One finds the usual man-produced pollution where the trail drops to the river. Strewn about an old camping site are rusted tin cans, bottles, cast iron pans, dented pots, a rotting sleeping bag and other remnants, probably those of a past gold prospector. Once we made our way downriver, however, fighting through poison oak bushes and dense willow and alder masses, around massive boulders and cliffs, we fished waters seldom, if ever, touched by others. A raft carrying foolhardy individuals may pass through here once every few years or so, but few on foot.

In ensuing years, I returned to this wild place many times, often with one of the boys, sometimes alone. On several outings, Kirk and I packed in for a night, fishing the prime evening and morning hours.

Although we initially found the fishing just so-so, there was sufficient action to keep us coming back. Sometimes I wondered if we were catching the same fifteen trout each time. But fishing in rapturous solitude amply rewarded our efforts. And with moderate to low flows, this small river presented superb fly fishing stretches.

One time, tired from the hike and exertion put forth to reach the good runs, I took a seat on a warm, flat rock at the

head of a long pool. The flow entered here in a swift chute, creating a gush of white water before settling to calmness.

My first casts failed to raise a fish. I changed to a big bushy Sofa Pillow pattern and tossed it onto the water, feeding enough line to reach the pool's far end. I retrieved the fly against the current, and then repeated the sequence. Resting more than fishing, I sat there absorbed in the rugged beauty of the surroundings, with the canyon heat, droning of the river, and my own weariness leaving me in a mindless stupor.

On one retrieve, just as I was lifting the fly from the churning water, a fat rainbow shot out of the water like a missile, engulfing the fly in the air. The fish must have followed the fly while I was pulling it back, and when the large morsel of food was about to escape, the trout attacked it ferociously, taking the bushy pretender a good eighteen inches off the surface.

The rainbow came down with the fly hooked in its mouth, and then raced downstream like a nuclear submarine in full throttle. I allowed it to rip line from my reel to avoid a sudden stop. Now energized, I let the trout pull and tug at the end of my line. After a minute or so, I decided to bring it in. When I made my move, the fish, aided by the strong current, combated my efforts, and before I knew it I was holding a slack line.

Hindsight tells me I should have made my way poolside, where I could have brought the fish in with less struggle. Disappointed not to see this spirited creature up close, I took solace in knowing it escaped intact. It sure woke me up this day. How often does a fish jump straight up out of the water to take a fly?

That evening, a good insect hatch occurred in the pool near our camp. Kirk and I counted six smallish trout feeding off the water's surface. While I cooked dinner, Kirk succeeded in hooking all six before darkness. The river then serenaded us to sleep.

The Middle Fork held even more surprises. Kirk and I set out for the river in early May. The water level was ideal, the air clear and crisp. Arriving at our usual spot early afternoon, we split up, Kirk going upriver and me down. For the next two hours I had a fish strike my fly on nearly every cast. The river was loaded with fat trout, primarily ten- to thirteen-inch rainbows, each a tenacious fighter. By the time I stopped, I had hooked and released over two dozen fish. Kirk had also caught a bunch. We wondered where all of these trout had been hiding before this day.

While hiking out the next day, the canyon elements infused my mind. I thought how cleansing to the body and soul it is to tramp to a place few others get to, where bears and other wild creatures hang out, where the river's shores defy travel, where the water and air are clear, and where wild trout are thriving.

5
Unlocking Secrets: The Tuolumne

But today he only saw one of the river's secrets, one that gripped his soul. He saw that the water continually flowed and flowed and yet it was always there; it was always the same and yet every moment it was new. Who could understand, conceive of this? He did not understand it; he was only aware of a dim suspicion, a faint memory, divine voices.—**Herman Hesse, Siddhartha.**

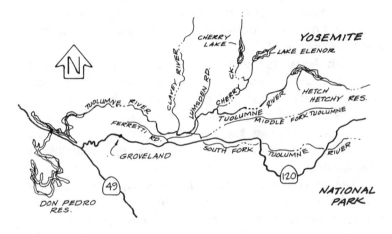

The 158-mile Tuolumne River begins with two small streams tumbling down the slopes of Mount Dana and Mount Lyell, the two largest mountains in Yosemite National Park. The two forks—Dana and Lyell—join at Tuolumne Meadows to form the Tuolumne River. After meandering through the meadows, the river plunges twenty-five miles through the Grand Canyon of the Tuolumne. The infamous O'Shaughnessy Dam, a structure John Muir vigorously fought, halts the river's natural flow, creating the Hetch Hetchy Reservoir that filled a valley comparable in grandeur to Yosemite Valley. In 1984, the eighty-three-mile stretch of Tuolumne from its headwaters to the Don Pedro Reservoir, forty-five miles downriver from Hetch Hetchy, was designated a National Wild and Scenic River, thus preserving it from further degradation.

Miwok Indians inhabited the Tuolumne River watershed for thousands of years. Over 250 archeological sites and other artifacts still exist in the river canyon. "Tuolumne" originates from the Indian word, "talmalamne," meaning a cluster of stone houses or caves.

The hordes of gold seekers who stampeded to California's foothills in 1849 to make their fortunes ravaged the area, including the Tuolumne. With each passing decade the methods to uncover the increasingly harder-to-find gold deposits grew more and more environmentally disruptive. Old mines, equipment and structures from the gold-mining era are still visible up and down the canyon.

With the white man's onslaught, the Miwoks suffered the abuse and demise common to Native Americans throughout the country. Between 1845 and 1900 their numbers declined to 700 from a prior population of 9000. Today the Bureau of Indian Affairs estimates there are 2,000 full- or half-blooded Miwok Indians, indicating a reinvigoration for these native people.

The lower canyon of the Tuolumne supports a tightly-webbed biosphere of life, missed by casual observation. Many of the mammals such as raccoons, gray fox and bobcats are primarily nocturnal. So too are rattlesnakes in the heat of summer. Some animal and amphibian species survive the summer heat by entering a torpid state called "estivation"—the summer equivalent of hibernation. Others such as mountain lions, black bear, coyotes and deer migrate to the higher, cooler elevations.

The sunny southern slopes require plants and trees capable of surviving with minimal water during the summer months. These include buck brush, Foothill pine, mountain mahogany, holly leaf and the widespread chamise ground cover. Along the river banks, willows, alders, bayleaves, blackberries and wild grape present a dense profusion of riparian plant life. The blackberry and wild grape represent non-native, introduced species.

The small wrentits, canyon wrens, black phoebes and swallows, the pervasive jays, woodpeckers and California quail, and the larger hawks, vultures and eagles, along with the countless varieties of insects, all occupy crucial places in this intricately woven ecosystem. So too do suckers, squawfish and wild trout.

Getting Hooked

Almost everything about the Tuolumne River is difficult. Except for the section in Tuolumne Meadows, car access is limited. In the lower canyon—setting for the renowned whitewater rafting runs—cliffs, steep hillsides, huge boulders and dense brush encase the river, effectively keeping all but the most persistent foot travelers away. Summer days are usually blistering. The river's churning, boulder-strewn waters flip many a raft. Despite it all, the Tuolumne is by far my favorite.

It took a while before the river's magic took hold of me. I first visited it on a raft trip. Called the "champagne of western rivers," and one of the most technical of all rivers to raft, the Tuolumne had long been on my "must do" list. Early on I persuaded some friends to join me on a private trip led by experienced guides.

A drive down Lumsden Road, the means of access to the rafting put-in, itself is a courageous act. As our van bounced and rattled down this narrow, twisting, rocky dirt road chiseled out of the side of the canyon, we glimpsed snakelike sections of river far below. When we saw oscillating masses of whitewater punctuating the river's flow at regular intervals, the undigested breakfasts still high in a few chests almost saw daylight again.

The Tuolumne's whitewater that day provided us with a one-of-a-kind experience. A flip by one of our rafts on Clavey Falls, one of the most renowned rapids in western rivers, added more drama than some of us desired, especially for the female passenger who, after the boat toppled, remained in an eddy holding a piece of rock wall with nothing but churning whitewater every place she looked. Nevertheless, rafting the "T" proved even more exhilarating than we had imagined.

After this initial voyage, a few years elapsed before I returned, this time to see how the fishing was. Kirk and I headed to the river on a hot mid-July day. We drove down Lumsden Road, named for two brothers who carved out a pathway during the 1890's to drive cattle down to the river to reach the grassy meadows in the national forests above the upper Tuolumne Canyon. In the 1930's, the Civilian Conservation Corps transformed this trail into the "road" it is today. Ranchers still drive herds of cattle down and back up what was called the Lumsden Trail. On more than one frustrating occasion I've had to stop my car and wait for hundreds of cows to pass.

On this particular day, Kirk and I saw a camper at the Lumsden Falls campground, holding what looked to be a string of trout. We strolled over to him and were stunned to see a single, large rainbow. As we talked, another fisherman came by and he too had a large trout.

"I fish here every year at this time," the first fisherman said. "Big rainbows are moving upriver, stopping below the falls."

These trout weighed between three and four pounds—not your typical Sierra fish. Kirk and I hurried to set up our gear, eager to catch one of these trophies.

We saw four more large rainbows caught by other fishermen that day, all on artificial bait such as salmon eggs, power bait and the like. This should have been our cue something was amiss. These lunkers seemed far too accommodating for large *wild* trout.

In our customary manner, Kirk and I hiked away from the bridge area to a distant stretch of river, and managed to hook only a couple of small trout. Nonetheless, as we drove home, we were convinced that we had finally discovered a Sierra river capable of yielding big wild trout.

Hopes high, we returned to the Tuolumne time and time

again. We fished it hard, up and down the rugged shoreline, with flies, grasshoppers, nightcrawlers, and lures. Casting flies on hot summer days in furnace-like temperatures proved futile and tormenting. The water always looked promising but our catches continued to be small and sparce.

Repeatedly, we drove back up dusty Lumsden Road, hot and tired, discouraged by another poor fishing outing. Like most rivers, the Tuolumne was requiring dues from us before giving up its secrets.

The more I fished the Tuolumne the more convinced I became something was wrong about the lunker trout we saw caught that first July day. Wild trout don't gorge on artificial bait. The California Department of Fish and Game confirmed my suspicions that these fish were not wild but rather hatchery-reared "broodstock" rainbows stocked in the pool below Lumsden Falls.

I wasn't ready to give up on the Tuolumne however. I became even more allied with its well being after learning the Modesto and Turlock irrigation districts had applied for federal permits to construct a dam and diversion project in the Tuolumne Canyon—a development that would flood this canyon just like the Stanislaus. The year was 1984, bringing with it another threat from Big Brother.

Never Could We Ever Recreate It.

Remembering the loss of the Stanislaus, supporters of wild rivers rallied to protect the Tuolumne. The Tuolumne River Preservation Trust (TRPT) was formed, adopting the strategy that the best defense is a good offense. TRPT, led by John Amodio, campaigned to bring the Tuolumne into the National Wild and Scenic River System, safeguarding it from future development. Dam proponents included powerful Congressman Tony Coelho, who represented the Modesto Irrigation District.

I enlisted in the campaign, committed to do as much as I could to avoid losing another one of my favorite rafting and fishing rivers. My first effort was to organize a public gathering in Palo Alto, featuring a talk by John Amodio and a slide presentation by river photographer Don Briggs. I next scheduled a meeting with my Congressman, Ed Zschau, who also represented part of Stanislaus County. His support was crucial. Bob Hackamack, one of the original rafters of the Tuolumne, and Los Altos Mayor, Roy Lave, a friend of Zschau, joined me at this meeting. Zschau was impressed with our case and the depth of support for the Tuolumne, and later came out in favor of a wild and scenic designation.

Amodio asked me to represent fishing interests at the upcoming hearing in Washington D.C. before the Subcommittee on Public Lands and National Parks of the House Committee on Interior and Insular Affairs. Many there with a stake in the well-being of the Tuolumne spoke on behalf of the river.

. Amodio's statement included the following:

The Tuolumne River is a vital part of the life of California. Its future will be decided by this Congress. As you know, the Toulumne River has a special place in the heritage and history of America's conservation movement. It has also always had a special relationship with Congress.

At the turn of the century, John Muir and a fledgling conservation movement waged one of the country's first public campaigns to preserve a unique part of the American landscape, the grandeur of the Tuolumne River's Hetch Hetchy Valley. They lost, and two major dams were built within Yosemite National Park to give San Francisco cheap water and electricity. Simultaneous to granting San Francisco the extraordinary privilege of building a dam within a national park, Congress dedicated the Tuolumne as a multiple-use river.

The Tuolumne River remains an incomparable example of wild America's rich environmental heritage. On the Tuolumne we are extremely fortunate to find—already in place—that highly valued balance between human needs and environmental integrity which is the supreme goal of all who seek to mediate between conservation and development.

In fact, the Tuolumne is living proof that such a balance can exist in a complex modern society. Wild and Scenic designation will formalize that balance. It will dedicate 83 miles of the main

stem to recreational use and natural values as documented to be its highest and best public use. The Tuolumne is a superlative recreational resource and national asset which we cannot afford to sacrifice.

Richard Chamberlain, the actor and wild river advocate, delivered the most moving testimony.

When I was a little kid, I loved to look through our family photo album. I was especially intrigued by pictures of my grandfather and my grandmother, who were both master trout fisherman, practicing their art in their turn-of-the-century fishing garb. I also got into a lot of trouble playing with my grandfather's fascinating fishing gear which was stored in our garage.

Last year when I told my dad I was going to Washington to lobby for the Tuolumne River, he excitedly told me that the Tuolumne was, in fact, my grandparents' favorite place to camp and fish. So unbeknownst to me, the magnificent Tuolumne River was in my blood long before I fell in love with her.

Three years ago some friends and I rafted down the incomparable whitewater of the Tuolumne. What thrilling days those were. And the evenings, camping along the river's banks, were equally wonderful in their serenity and breathtaking beauty. After the chaotic hubbub of city life, we all felt deeply refreshed. The river itself has a presence, a power that makes you feel close to the very source of nature, of life.

This magnificent river does not belong to two irrigation districts, nor does it belong just to California. The Tuolumne is a national treasure. And a hard-working treasure at that. The Tuolumne's five dams provide two percent of California's electricity, they irrigate hundreds of thousands of acres of agricultural land, and supply water to one of every 12 homes in the state.

And yet, amazingly, 83 miles of free-flowing river and wilderness remain unharmed.

And here, I think, is the real issue. The Tuolumne can serve our whole country as a splendid example of the nearly perfect balanced use of a superb natural resource. Further development will turn the river into a single purpose energy mine.

To my eyes, God seems to have a lavished a special abundance of living gifts on the Tuolumne River and its surrounding wilderness. We have power to destroy it, but never, never in our wildest imagination could we ever recreate it.

Chamberlain's statement capstoned the victory. Congress bestowed "wild and scenic" status on the Tuolumne in 1984 as part of the California Wilderness Bill.

The outpouring of support on behalf of the Tuolumne showed that environmental advocacy could translate into political clout. Then Senator Pete Wilson, a politician who represents anti-environmental interests more than pro-environmental interests, reportedly received more letters on this issue than any other while senator. The letters persuaded him to join Senator Alan Cranston in supporting wild and scenic designation for the Tuolumne thereby producing the needed support of the two California senators. My own involvement in this successful fight sealed the growing bond between me and the river.

It All Comes Together

Convinced the Tuolumne held a robust population of wild trout, and captivated by its beauty, relative obscurity and challenging fishing, I repeatedly returned to its shores. I hiked upriver above Lumsden Falls in terrain requiring jungle survival skills. I routinely crossed Meral's Pool—the rafting put-in pool—in a small raft to reach the southern, less vegetated side, and then hiked far downriver on an old trail maintained by feral cows. Using flies in most runs, but resorting to an occasional nightcrawler in the deeper holes, I succeeded in catching trout, with many in the eleven- to thirteen-inch range and an occasional fifteen-inch specimen. My persistence was beginning to pay off.

My confidence that I could catch trout in all kinds of water by fly fishing eventually increased to the extent I dropped for good the use of my old standby—nightcrawlers. I was free, at last, but perhaps freed from more than just using bait. How I caught trout had become as important to me as how many I caught.

My knowledge of the river grew. In one particular pool three miles down from Meral's, I frequently raised a good trout while fishing it on my way downriver, and then again coming back. It represents a wonderful piece of holding water. A long, tumbling rapid carries food down to the pool. Large, submerged boulders provide the trout with protecting lies. Varied currents sweep through the run presenting feeding lanes and drift lines.

In order to get back to my car before dark, I usually had to leave this pool just when the trout were becoming active, reminding me of New Zealand when I discovered night fishing. On one trip I looked around and saw an ideal camping spot. I thought, instead of hauling myself out like I usually do, I could stay and fish right up 'til dark. I'd never camped by myself out in the wild before, but why not?

I left that day intent on spending the night alongside this pool my next time out. When I did weeks later, I discovered what I had suspected—the trout were biting when I normally would be hoofing it back to my car. That evening I enjoyed the best two hours of fishing ever on the Tuolumne. I got in my sleeping bag that night feeling pretty damn smart and a tad adventuresome. And I wasn't even scared when it got dark.

It makes sense to be on a productive piece of water when the fishing is apt to be best, usually in the evening or early morning. But how often does a person fish a remote section of a river at one of these times? Further, who knows when fish will go on an aggressive bite? Insect hatches are a reliable predictor but there are other, more mysterious factors at work. What are they? Drastic change in weather or temperature? Dropping barometer? Cloudy night? Any fisherman knows that fish will sometimes go on an aggressive feed when no apparent elements are obvious. By camping on the river, I was there *whenever the trout decided to bite*. Not a sophisticated strategy, but an effective one nonetheless.

Tuolumne trout taught me that fish might become active at any time—morning, noon or night. Likewise, they could be "down" at any time—a state far more frequent than the former. Plus, I couldn't predict with certainty one or the other circumstance. I would experience a great evening of fishing up to the onset of darkness, and then find the river totally "off" the next evening. Same place, time and conditions. Of course, it's this unpredictability that makes fishing what it is.

Most times when I camped and fished the Tuolumne, I returned to this spot. For me it had everything: a great shade tree, a flat area to lay my sleeping bag, large rocks to place items on and sit against, and above all, a long run of water holding numerous trout. The numerous Indian grinding holes nearby suggest the Miwoks liked this location as well.

With each visit, I simplified practicalities, such as eating and sleeping, to maximize time spent fishing. In the morning I would consume juice and a muffin or two. For lunch I'd eat variations of cheese and crackers, fruit, hard-boiled eggs, trail mix, and celery sticks filled with peanut butter. For dinners, I carried ready-made food: snack items, deli sandwiches, burritos, containers of salad, and despite their nutritional liabilities, some cream-filled, chocolate-covered, and jelly-filled items. And of course I brought beer. I lugged in a small ice chest holding an ice block, cumbersome to carry, but worth the effort. Few things equal an ice cold drink after a hot, strenuous day.

For summertime sleeping, I left my sleeping bag at home in favor of a plastic-coated space blanket. For the balmy canyon nights, I required no cover at all, except perhaps in the early-morning hours. I did indulge in a thick air mattress rather than the thin backpacking version. It was more weight to pack in, but like the ice, worth it.

All of the rewards from my Tuolumne excursions came together one memorable August trip. I arrived at my pool early afternoon, and immediately experienced good fishing. The trout were in that wonderful mode of hitting flies quick and hard.

After the fish had stopped biting, I continued casting a brightly colored fly over and over, mindlessly watching it drift down the current. I was startled out of my trance by a crested meganser duck with her brood of six ducklings motoring down the far side of the pool. Appreciatively I watched them scoot downriver.

Taking a mid-afternoon break, I settled down on a sandy spot shaded by an oak tree with a rock to serve as a backrest. While I sat there, red, white and black hairy woodpeckers flying about the opposite hillside, and pecking at dead tree trunks, kept me in an hypnotic state. Nearby, full-bodied, black bumblebees buzzed around a blooming button bush. Nature's interlocking magic was never more evident than when bees alighted on the spherical, pin-cushion-like, white blossoms to gather nectar.

In the fading afternoon sunlight, insects covered the pool, causing it to resemble a shimmering, golden desert. Dragon flies jetted about, touching down every few seconds as if to grab a sip of liquid. A trout launched itself two feet out of the water trying to nab one of these aerial acrobats.

Come evening the fish became active again, and kept feeding up to the onset of darkness. The day's total included four fish in the fifteen- to seventeen-inch range and a half dozen from ten to fourteen inches, all taken on dry flies.

The hot sand and warm granite rock felt good as I plunked myself down at day's end. A gentle, balmy breeze wafted up the canyon. The Fosters Lager was ice cold, my turkey sandwich thick and moist, a three-bean salad sweet and tangy. I lingered over every tasty morsel, feeling thoroughly refreshed and content. Later, stars covered the black heavens and serenading cicadas filled the air waves. The constant drum of the shimmering Tuolumne nearby provided a melodic backdrop.

The next morning, after hooking a couple more robust rainbows, I packed up and left. Things had coalesced for me on this trip. I felt refreshed, energized, attuned to nature and my deepest values. The Tuolumne's sounds, fragrances and images remained fixed in my senses for days and weeks afterwards.

Spaced Out

I set my backpack down at my camping spot late this cloudy June afternoon, anxious as always to start fishing. For the next two hours, I didn't get a single strike.

The skies were darkening. I put the rod down, went to my ice chest and pulled out dinner. With a king-sized can of Bud in one hand and a giant chicken burrito in the other, I sunk into the sand, my back against a boulder. The air had turned cool.

"Damn!" I said when the first raindrops started pelting my bare arms. I hadn't planned for rain. The high river flow prevented me from crossing the river to get to the other side and the trail back to my car. I was stuck here wondering how I left weather out of my calculations.

I dug in my backpack for the wool shirt I throw in for such situations. It wasn't there. Convinced it's always hot and dry in the canyon during the summer, I had neglected to bring any warm clothing. I also didn't bring a sleeping bag, opting instead for just a space blanket—one side plastic and the other a silver foil. I did bring a thin plastic sheet to serve as a tarp in the "remote chance of rain."

The rain started falling in earnest. I wrapped my space blanket around me and hastily gathered firewood. I got a small flame going among twigs but the driving rain quickly doused it.

I got the plastic sheet out of my pack and rigged up a flimsy lean-to shelter by tying two corners on tree branches and placing rocks on the other two corners on the ground. Wrapped in my blanket I then hunkered down under the cover, rain now coming down in sheets. *This is going to be one long miserable night* I thought, and it wasn't even dark yet.

Wearing only two short-sleeved cotton shirts, and long pants, I laid down, covered myself with the space blanket, and tried to sleep, about as comfortable as a hairless Chihuahua in a metal cage. The problem was I wasn't at all tired.

The space blanket was soon doing its job of capturing the warmth of my body by reflecting it back. But the king-sized beverage I had earlier consumed produced a king-sized need to urinate. When I got up in the rainy night to relieve myself, the plastic blanket wrapped around me, the stored warmth in my little cocoon was lost.

It was back to my nest, tight fetal position, trying to warm up again, and fall asleep. Unfortunately the large mass of beer in my stomach pressing against my bladder combined with the cool air produced another need to urinate. And then again, and again, and again. I was not a happy camper.

The rain stopped sometime around midnight, having drenched everything—branches, ground, tarp. Water had beaded up on one side of my blanket, preventing me from wrapping it snugly around me. My mattress was damp. Yet, at this point, although I wasn't toasty warm, I wasn't cold.

If this rain storm had dropped down from Alaska, or if I had gotten my clothes soaked, I could have been in trouble from hypothermia. I was thinking that, while I may be uncomfortable I was not yet in any danger. If I could only fall asleep, I could get through the night in good shape. However, I didn't even doze. The hours passed.

At 3:30 a.m., I felt my first shiver. Not a good signal. I tucked my knees as tight against my chest as I could and wrapped my arms around them. But my store of heat-generating energy was all used up and I couldn't ward off the coolness enveloping my body. To try to start a fire at this time would have been futile. I lay there getting increasingly chilled.

Enough of this! I finally concluded. I sprang up and vigorously started doing calisthenics: sit-ups, push-ups, jumping jacks, running in place, more push-ups. I dug in my pack for an energy bar my wife had made consisting of figs, dried apricots and raisins all blended together with peanut butter to form a dense, carbohydrate-rich mass. I bit off quantities of the glop, filling my jowls like a squirrel. I did more calisthenics, all the while chewing and ingesting the glue-like substance.

My strategy worked. Blood rushed throughout my body creating much needed warmth. I swallowed the rest of the stuff still stuck to the insides of my mouth and went back to my enclave. I settled once again under my space blanket and closed my eyes, now feeling warm and relaxed. When I next looked up, it was morning. I packed up, crossed the river during the low morning flows, and hiked the three miles back to my car.

The next winter, Kirk gave me an army survival shirt for Christmas.

An Awakening

It was a crisp, clear autumn day in the Tuolumne Canyon. Yellow-leafed oaks, willows and alders, and red poison oak bushes, lined the canyon sides. The trout were active. To me this is the best time of the year to be in the outdoors.

On this day, Jim, an infrequent fishing buddy, joined me. Dark haired and lanky, this high school history teacher is an enthusiastic recreationist. He had been one of my most accommodating, energetic and enjoyable rafting companions throughout the early years of my whitewater trips.

Enroute to the Tuolumne, we stopped at a general store in Chinese Camp, a small town in the foothills, where Jim bought nightcrawlers. Later, when he opened the container down in the canyon, he found it filled with rotten crawlers. In a dubious win for free enterprise, the store proprietor had switched containers. Jim thought they "would work just as well."

On this day, Jim arranged a foul-smelling nightcrawler on his hook, tossed the glob into a deep pool, and had a very large fish engulf it. Letting out a loud whoop, he tried to lift the lunker up to the rock ledge where he stood only to see a big sucker flop back into the water. What else would consume such bait?

In the bright midday sun, Jim and I proceeded downriver. I wore my warm weather attire: shorts, tee shirt, fishing vest and sneaks with no socks. This being the last weekend in October, I half thought rattlesnake season was past, consequently I was not focused on where I stepped as I customarily am in river canyons. In the lead, I moved swiftly across a rock embankment with that confidence a foothold will always be there.

"Bob!" shouted Jim. "You just stepped right next to a huge snake."

I stopped and looked back. "What kind?"

"I don't know, it's yellow and brown."

"Probably a gopher snake. Let me have a look."

I retraced my steps and looked down on the largest rattlesnake I had ever seen. It was coiled near an inclined rock, basking in the sun. I must have stepped right next to it seconds earlier. What if I had stepped on it? It was not a thought I wanted to entertain.

The fearsome but impressive creature appeared asleep. I moved closer. Its massive, diamond-shaped head was flattened against its thick, scaled body. Its yellow eyes with metallic-colored specks and vertical black slots for pupils projected a vacant, expressionless stare as I stood peering at it from thirty inches away.

My first impulse was to kill the monster. One less deadly rattler in my fishing grounds seemed like a good thing. Plus, the skin would make quite a trophy. I went looking for something to crush its head, and returned with two large stones.

"Be careful Bob, that's a big snake," Jim said, backing up.

I raised one stone above my head and sent it crashing towards the reptile. It angled off the inclined side of the rock sheltering the snake and bounced away. The rattler didn't budge. I heaved the second rock and it too ricocheted away without touching the slumbering giant.

Gripping a third missile, I carefully aimed it before hurling it down. Again the rock hit the inclined side of the granite, missed the snake, and clanged off. At this point the rattler woke up.

I'm not sure what would have happened if the snake took the offensive. I probably would have scaled the tops of a few rocks before jumping into the river. Fortunately the giant rattler exhibited only one desire—to get back to its den. Five feet of undulating body uncoiled, the reptile slithering up the hillside into a crevice. It never showed any aggression. Only after it was deep in its refuge did I hear its tail buzzing.

Some time after meeting this creature, and encountering a few more rattlesnakes elsewhere, my outlook changed. I had killed several rattlers, mostly small- and medium-sized specimens. I had my trophy snake skin displayed at the cabin. But understanding slowly began percolating up to my brain on the harm I was inflicting on what I valued most—wilderness.

Rattlesnakes are vital creatures in nature. So too are mountain lions, grizzlies, owls, hawks, coyotes and wolves. They are allies in keeping wild trout habitat healthy and thriving. When predatory species decline, other species multiply. Rattlesnakes keep rodent populations under control. I don't like excessive numbers of mice and ground squirrels scurrying around my camping area, getting into my pack and food, and spreading diseases. But most important, rattlesnakes, like all creatures in the natural realm, deserve to live regardless of how they impact *Homo sapiens*.

Not one rattlesnake I had ever encountered acted aggressively, except the one or two caught in vulnerable positions. And then it was a defensive posture. Not one ever took the opportunity to strike although some could easily have done so. Instead they sought to remain unobtrusive and undetected, or to retreat to safety. Rattlesnakes do their best to avoid man. Further, when I visit the places where they hang out, *I am the intruder, the guest.* I am ashamed at having been such a poor one.

I've returned to the Tuolumne many times since that trip with Jim, most often alone. One time after arriving at my favorite pool and setting up camp, I took a short walk. About fifty feet or so from my sleeping area, I happened to look under a large rock in a grassy area and discovered a neighbor. Shaded from the sun, curled like a length of thick rope, a large rattlesnake had found an ideal resting spot. I crouched and studied the snake, watching its tongue flick in and out as it attempted to evaluate my presence. We remained at peace and let the other be.

I returned a few weeks later and again saw my colleague napping under the same rock. The inside of this rock structure is its den. Now each time I return to the Tuolumne, I look for it, and am disappointed if it's not there.

What is this relationship all about? It's not much different from the relationship I have with wild trout. It has taken me years to learn that we're all in this together.

Dick's Introduction

After a fishing excursion, I'd often tell Dick, a close friend and tennis partner, about it. Dick was a stockbroker whom I usually called most days to check on stock quotes, mainly just to chat. I sometimes tried to coax him into joining me on a fishing outing. He typically mumbled something about being busy, but in truth I didn't think he was interested in the outdoors. He never told me that he had camped and fished throughout his early adult years.

After numerous invitations, Dick finally agreed to accompany me on a trip. I planned a one-day excursion to the Tuolumne and my favorite spot. I didn't tell him hiking was involved.

The July day we chose was one of the hottest days of the summer with the temperature exceeding 100 degrees down in the canyon. Per my usual routine, I planned on crossing the river in my small raft and then hiking down to my spot. When I inflated the dinghy this day, I failed to tightly secure the air valve and the raft slowly deflated as we crossed Meral's pool.

Dick could not swim well and became quite concerned. When he leaned to one side of our spongy craft, his brand-new Swiss army knife and bottle of salmon eggs dropped from his vest pockets into the water's depths. Despite his protests that I was trying to drown him, we made it safely to the other side.

On the hike downriver, after a half mile, Dick developed a bad blister on his big toe. Now limping, he moaned and cursed as we traversed the crumbling dirt hillside, tramped through poison oak and under low branches that snagged our hats and daypacks, dropping leaves and twigs down the back of our shirts.

Dick's face turned crimson in the day's searing heat. A white spittle formed at the corners of his parched mouth. At the halfway point, he slumped to the ground and cried out, "Madgic, I'll never forgive you for this." We pushed on.

When we reached my pool, Dick collapsed in a heap, saying "That's it, I'm not taking another step." I thought he was going to pass out. After resting, we ate our lunch in the shade. A gentle and cooling breeze drifted up the canyon.

Dick sat and watched as I set up my rod and started casting a fly about the pool, managing to hook and release four nice rainbows in about thirty minutes. I reeled in and told him I was going downriver. I left him readying his spinning rod, grousing about not having his salmon eggs.

I returned late afternoon to find Dick sitting on a rock. He said he had caught one fish and lost four spinning lures on snags. A chain held the fish captive in the water.

"You're keeping it?" I asked.

"What's the point of fishing if you don't keep the fish?" he responded.

"I fish just for the sport," I said. "Plus it won't be there to catch again."

He pondered my words for a few seconds and then said, "Well, since my wife and I don't like fish, I guess I'll let it go. I was going to give it to my cat."

We relaxed in the cooling afternoon shadows. Dick said, "This is really a beautiful spot. I enjoyed being here all afternoon whether I caught any fish or not. But there must be a better way to get here." He eyed the side of the canyon as though visualizing a tramway. Dick didn't grasp that if it were easy to reach this place, it would lose much of what makes it so special to me.

Before leaving, Dick made a few casts with my fly rod and hooked a small rainbow. He appeared pleased.

On the drive home, Dick confessed that he hated physical exertion. Although he played lots of tennis and golf, and looked to be in shape, it was discomfort he couldn't tolerate. He told me how much he disliked having to bend under the low branches on the trail. I told him pushing his body was a good way to become physically fit and added to the sport.

"I'd rather spend my time fishing," he said.

An unexpected result from this trip was that Dick became a convert to fly fishing. And like most converts, he became a fanatic. Within a few months he had outfitted himself with the best fly fishing equipment and clothing money could buy, had enrolled in fly casting lessons, and had joined the San Jose Flycasters Club. He also took up fly tying with a vengeance.

Dick thought nothing of spending hundreds of dollars on materials to make a few dozen flies for his next outing. One month, it was striped bass in a large reservoir, the next month it was trout or black bass in a lake, then it was off to Venezuela for bone fishing. He became an expert fly tier, turning out hundreds of beautifully crafted flies.

Dick's aversion to physical exertion never abated. Unconvinced of the merits of fishing the hard-to-get places, he fished as close to the car as possible. "Why waste time walking?" he would say.

A discussion about investing we had one time revealed our divergent outlooks. Dick asked me whether I get more upset when the stock market plummets and I'm caught holding losses, or when the market shoots up and I'm not fully invested.

I get more upset, I told him, when I don't participate in an up market, when I miss a good opportunity. Dick, on the other hand, said he always looked at the downside risks. If the market dropped sharply and he had losses, he was more upset than when he missed the profits of a rising market.

These differing investment approaches helped explain our respective attitudes towards outdoor excursions. First and foremost, I think of the prospects for good fishing and less of the possible downsides. Long drives, rough terrain and arduous hikes are investments for the rewards of even a half day of trout fishing on a wilderness stream.

When Dick considered a fishing venture, he would ponder how long the drive was, what the weather might be, how far he might have to walk. If any of these downside factors appeared too weighty, he would choose not to go.

Regardless of Dick's steadfast attitude I was determined to have him put on a backpack and join me for a night on the river. I knew he would enjoy it if I could just get him there, even if I had to hire an helicopter for him.

Meanwhile, Dick tried to persuade me to break out of my love affair with wild trout. "There's different kinds of fly fishing out there," he said. "Salt water, lakes...you need to branch out."

Before either of us convinced the other, Dick's time ran out.

We returned to the Tuolumne together one last time. Dick had just had another operation to remove cancerous tumors from his neck. The year before doctors had identified lingering sores on his scalp as basal cell cancer and had surgically removed them. In the ensuing months, the cancer had spread to his neck area, and doctors now diagnosed the cancer as the more virulent squamish cell cancer. Had the original diagnosis been accurate, doctors could have eradicated the cancer through radiation.

So Dick wasn't in the best physical condition on this day, weak from several operations, fresh scar tissue on his neck and back. He fished near the car, attempting with his typical determination to get a trout he saw to take his fly. "It's right there," he said. "I should get it to bite."

On our way home Dick mentioned this may be his last fishing trip. I had hoped, as did he, that the surgery had removed the tumors for good. The odds weren't good, however. After doing everything in his power to improve his chances, Dick accepted his fate with his customary grace and equanimity. He never expressed outrage about the hospital's error and how it had cost him his life. "It's a lousy way to die," was all he said.

The following spring, at 56 years of age, Dick died.

Dick was one of the most sensitive and generous individuals I have ever known. As he lay in his bed, suffering a slow, horrible death, he made sure his lovely wife, Earlene, sent flowers to my mother who had just lost her husband, my father. That's the kind of person he was. I loved the man.

I regret not having expressed myself more when he was alive, telling him how much I treasured his friendship and company, how I always looked forward to sharing my fishing experiences with him. Despite our differences, we always had a good time together. His death left a void in my life.

Dick was anticipating retirement and many years of leisure and fly fishing at the time the cancer took hold. He started fly fishing that first trip with me to the Tuolumne. It was the last place he fished. In my mind, Dick's spirit is still there.

Committing

On an early September day, I arrived at my favorite spot shortly before noon. I prepared my rod to limber up my casting before lunch. With the sun beating down on the low water, I didn't expect any action until later in the day.

I put on an Elk Hair Caddis dry, sending the fly out to some swirling water near a rock. Within seconds a strong thirteen-inch rainbow slammed the fly. For the next thirty minutes, a fish tore into my fly on just about every cast. Moving upriver, I continued to get savage strikes. The action didn't cool off until it was 2:30 p.m., a half mile from my first cast. I never once thought of lunch. Unfortunately this wondrous afternoon was soon to be ruined.

Up ahead, four guys were hauling a raft down a rocky stretch of river. Once past the rocks, they set the raft on the bank and two of them got out fishing rods. One passed me heading downriver with a spinning rod.

"We're waiting for the water to rise," he explained. "How's the fishing?"

After another hour or so, I reached the other fellow—a fly fisherman. He told me he had hooked and released "a few." As I made my way back, the first fisherman appeared with a string of trout, including some beauties.

"Look what I got," he shouted.

I almost lost it. Many of the precious wild rainbows I had earlier caught and released were probably on that string of dead fish. With as much edge to my voice as I could muster, I shouted back to him: "I put back the fish I caught."

"It's hard to throw them back when you use nightcrawlers," he said sheepishly.

Fuming, I turned away, saying nothing.

I agonized over the incident all weekend. The trout are too vulnerable when the water is low and they're on a bite. No river can take the kind of harvesting of wild fish I had witnessed. I made a personal pledge to do something.

The river level never rose that day. I took some solace in watching the boaters lug their big raft up the canyon's steep side. I'm not sure the string of rainbows survived the trek out. What did the guy plan on doing with all those fish?

I've seen other fishermen on the Tuolumne, armed with bait or hardware, hauling out strings of big wild trout. The U.S. Forest Service had built a new trail from Meral's Pool to Clavey Falls—six miles downriver, opening the river to more fishermen. Tuolumne trout needed to be protected and I was determined to do something about it.

I contacted Dave Lentz, a Wild Trout Coordinator at the California Department of Fish and Game (DFG) and told him about the unrestricted harvesting of wild trout from the Tuolumne. "It's rare to find a Sierra river with a population of big wild trout," I said. "Restrictions are needed."

Lentz heard me but couldn't act at first, due to tight budgets. A year passed, and after several more phone calls pleading my case, he placed a "Fisherman's Survey" box at the head of the new trailhead to gather needed information. Bill Lane of the Groveland Forest Service contributed important support and information.

After reviewing the data, and walking the new trail, Lentz concluded a western slope Sierra river holding large trout is indeed a unique and valuable resource and the Tuolumne's trout needed protection.

In 1995, the DFG, with the support of CalTrout and its president, Jim Edmundson, recommended to the California Fish and Game Commission that the Tuolumne be designated a "Wild Trout River," with regulations limiting trout taken to two fish *under* twelve inches. In 1994, the Commission accepted the recommendation.

Thank you, Dave Lentz for hearing and responding to my pleas. Thank you, Bill Lane, for jumping in and championing "your river." Thank you, Jim Edmundson and CalTrout, for getting out in front of this issue. From these collective efforts, Tuolumne's wild trout population can only get stronger.

Reflections

My Tuolumne site takes on many levels of personal meaning. At the most basic, it represents my favorite fishing pool and place to camp. I love how the water flows through the pool, creating the unique ebbs, runs and swirls I've gotten to know so well. I love standing on this rock, on that piece of shore, and making long casts to the prime holding spots of the trout.

I love the obscurity and character of this spot—where I sit under an oak tree, rest on the sand against a rock, lay my sleeping bag. I love knowing this place as intimately as I do, its many sides and moods that I've grown to trust and count on. Whenever I want to reduce stress, I visualize this spot in my mind. I see it, I hear the rapids, I feel the pull of the trout. It's comforting to have such a place to send my mind to every now and then.

When Diane and I first came west, and during our early family years, we traveled extensively, receiving tremendous enjoyment from our spectacular national parks and monuments. Since then, I've grown to value the finer, more delicate gifts of nature over the years: cascading water flowing into an alder-lined, green pool; bright red penstemon growing in cracks on a granite ledge along a stream; a water ouzel bobbing on a rock midstream; water from a spring trickling down a moss-covered bank; the smell of pine; the sounds of a woodpecker. I prefer now to return to the intricate beauty and peaceful solitude of such places.

At a deeper level, the connections I've established have become the most satisfying. As much as I love exploring new places, I have found greater satisfaction in giving myself deeply to one entity over prolonged time. The other creatures present here, the canyon breezes, the myriad of plants and insects, the constant presence of a river—I am connected to each and all of these elements. The rafters, fishermen and hikers who sometimes pass by, and who respect where they are, are part of this wilderness community. We are all joined together, connected by an unknown, but nevertheless felt, power.

By being part of the canyon community, I have come to know myself better. It is my own self-awareness, my own humanity, that I renew and extend by returning time after time. It is a place where I relax, reflect, achieve peace and contentment, and grow spiritually. Here, I am able to let go of fears and anxieties.

When I listen intently to the sounds of the river, I hear those calming soothing voices heard by Siddhartha. The difference between being alive and being joined with the canyon elements in death begins to blur, and I find death not to be so frightening.

The Tuolumne has revealed many secrets. As Siddhartha also discovered: *The river knows everything; one can learn everything from it.*

6
Renewal: The East Carson

To protect your rivers, protect your mountains.—**Chinese Emperor, 1600 B.C.**

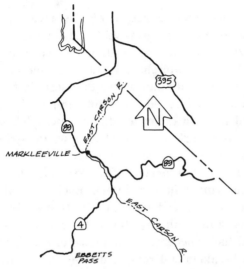

Originating at 10,000 feet in the Carson-Iceberg Wilderness on the eastern Sierra, and ending 125 miles later in the Carson Sink in Nevada, the East Carson is a river of many faces. Named in honor of Kit Carson, famed explorer and scout, the East Carson first plunges down the mountain slopes and carves through a long, narrow canyon before meeting Highway 4 east of the small town of Markleeville. Tributaries Wolf Creek and Silver Creek add substantially to the river's volume here. It then flows alongside Highway 89 for six miles before the road and river depart at Hangman's Bridge.

At Hangman's Bridge, the East Carson begins its twenty-two-mile journey through a multi-colored, high desert canyon before its flow is interrupted by the Ruhenstroth Dam in Gardnerville, Nevada. Foothill and Jeffrey pines grow on the hillsides, enshrouding the canyon with green and gray hues. Snow-capped Sierra peaks frame the western views.

East Carson Hot Springs is located approximately eight and a half miles from Hangman's Bridge. Here a hot creek and an inviting pool with a consistent temperature of 102 degrees sit near the river. Two miles further downriver, the East Carson leaves California and enters Nevada.

The caves and ledges along the river, particularly those near the hot springs, reveal signs of ancient dwellers. In the early 1800s, Washoe Indians moved in bands about the East Carson watershed. In the summer months, they ascended to the mountain where they hunted for deer and mountain sheep, foraged for edible and medicinal plants, and netted trout in the clear alpine waters. Their summer delicacy was a bark worm that they would string around their necks and east morsel by morsel.

When Autumn arrived, the Washoes left the high country to winter in the desert. Each year they would launch a rabbit drive, driving hundreds of rabbits into long grass nets and clubbing them to death. The Indians celebrated their successes with a feast of rabbit meat. They fashioned blankets and robes from the skins, often trading such wares with the Miwok and Maidu tribes for acorns or other items.

The first white man to explore the area was Jedediah Smith who crossed Ebbetts Pass in the spring of 1827. His arrival presaged the coming of many more whites and the eventual decline of the Washoe way of life.

With the gold rush of '49, hordes of white people descended upon the region. It wasn't gold mining, however, that ravaged the land this time. The discovery of silver a decade later did. At Virginia City, Nevada, the richest strike of silver ever made in the world occurred at the Comstock Lode and changed the character of the land forever.

The extraction of silver ore from the earth involved huge chambers supported by heavy wooden beams, thus producing an insatiable need for timber. Mining interests harvested all the forests within striking distance of the Comstock Lode, eventually cutting as much as 73,000,000 board feet of virgin timber from the lower Sierra. In one year, 250,000 board feet of cut wood floated down the East Carson to lumber mills. When the mining companies required more timber the loggers moved towards the headwaters of the East Carson higher in the Sierra. Today, although the forests in this region are again dense with tree growth, they consist of relatively young trees.

A map of this area in the late 1800s shows several lumber towns not there today: Silver Mountain, Centerville, Mt. Bullion, Monitor, Splinterville, Silver King. With the exception of the picturesque town of Markleeville, little evidence remains today of the other towns, or the footbridges, dams and tunnels constructed to support the pervasive mining formerly in the region. Through fires, floods and other natural events, Mother Nature gradually is restoring the region's natural grandeur.

First Exposure

"The water is forty two degrees. Fall in without wetsuits and you've got about ten seconds before hypothermia sets in." An experienced kayaker told me and my fellow rafters this just before we launched my new raft on the East Carson River in May, 1976.

On the international river runners scale of I to VI, where I is flat moving water and VI is unrunnable, the East Carson rates a Level II, meaning it has a swift current and sections of white water, but no deep drops or holes, no big standing waves, no major obstructions to navigate. In rafter's parlance, the East Carson is "a piece of cake." That's precisely why I chose it for the maiden voyage of my raft.

My companions on this day were a group of teachers from the high school where I was principal. Our prior rafting experience (non-commercial) consisted mainly of one trip with inexpensive rented rafts down the Stanislaus River. With the spongy boats, we flipped three times in the first four miles. The durable, stiff hypalon composition and eighteen-inch tubes of my new thirteen-foot Campways raft, prepared us for any whitewater challenge. Or so I thought.

Since we didn't have wet suits, the kayaker's statement sobered us somewhat, but we were not to be deterred. At the rafting put-in at Hangman's Bridge, we broke out a bottle of champagne to christen the boat's inauguration. Spirits high, we crashed through the first gush of white water on our way down river.

Although the East Carson does not contain big drops or troublesome obstacles, it does have abrupt turns and bends. At the half-mile mark, we confronted a sharp bend. The powerful current swept us toward a rock embankment with a low overhanging ledge. To avoid hitting the rock wall, I had to break out of the current and keep the boat in the center of the river. However I didn't yet know how to guide a raft to do this manuever.

Slamming into the rock wall wasn't the problem. White water rafting involves bouncing off rocks. The problem was the low overhanging ledge. As we plowed into the rocky craig, the three crew members on the right side of the raft tumbled over to the left side to avoid hitting their heads. Six persons all on one side of a six-person raft is poor technique. The raft flipped, dumping us into the forty-two-degree water.

One thousand one, one thousand two, one thousand three...

I managed to break out of the current and scramble to shore in eight seconds. Looking back, I saw four of my colleagues clambering up the bank.

The boat was floating down the river upside down, followed by our sixth crew member. After fifty yards or so, he was able to catch an eddy and crawl to shore. A kayaker grabbed our raft, paddles and supply bag.

Although this mishap unsettled us, we emerged more or less unscathed, discounting a few minor bruises and lacerations. One crew member experienced a mild case of shock, more from shaken nerves than from any physical injury. After twenty minutes in the hot sun wrapped in towels, even crew member number six eventually stopped shaking. We regrouped and carried out the rest of the trip flawlessly.

I never flipped a raft again. Although boatmates have on occasion been tossed overboard, my boat has always remained upright. Because of that singular experience on the East Carson, the river has been forever etched in my heart and memory.

Learning Slowly

I was unaware of the East Carson's wild trout potentials until I signed up for a high Sierra fishing trip led by Ralph Cutter, author of *Sierra Trout Guide*. Around the campfire, members of the group exchanged information on favorite fishing rivers. Ralph cited the East Carson, saying: "You won't catch a lot but the native trout are beautiful. The canyon is a lovely place to fish."

Ralph also spoke of the considerable abuse heaped on the East Carson over the years from characters who take out as many fish as they can, degrade the environment, and even go four-wheeling along the river's banks. Recalling my raft trip there, I decided this unique river canyon warranted another visit.

The next summer, Kirk and I drove over Ebbetts Pass to check out East Carson trout. We continued west on Highway 89 past Markleeville looking for a place to hike to the river. We found a dirt road that took us to the base of the low mountain range eclipsing the river canyon. After parking, we scanned the ridgeline and spotted a low saddle. We put our daypacks on and hiked to it. We then followed a dry creek bed down from the ridge. After thirty minutes of tramping in loose shale and sand, we glimpsed the tea-colored East Carson chugging along the canyon bottom.

When we reached the river, we set up our rods and worked our way downstream. After one hour, we only had one small rainbow to show for our efforts. We passed over many wide, shallow stretches of river that didn't hold trout. But then the river would be squeezed between rock walls, causing it to curve and twist snakelike before forming a deep pool. The pinkish cliffs and grottos looked like a creative child had molded them from clay and pebbles.

In a shallow, braided section of river, I landed a fat, scrappy thirteen-inch rainbow. Ralph Cutter was correct: the fish was beautiful, more silvery than other rainbows I've seen. Our spirits picked up.

From a deeper pool, Kirk brought in an eleven-inch beauty and then another. I hooked two more. By day's end, we had caught and released nine fish, all wild rainbows. We drove home pleased at having located another river holding robust wild trout.

For my next visit to the East Carson, I coaxed Jim, a close friend and longtime outdoors companion (different "Jim" from the Tuolumne adventure), to join me. This time we would backpack to the canyon and spend two nights, with the second by the hot springs. "It's only a few miles from where we hit the river," I told Jim.

An affable and accommodating person, Jim requires little convincing to join me on such excursions. Although he started fly fishing long before I did, he isn't as committed. The nuances of rods, lines, flies and leaders don't interest him much. He instead prefers the rigors of the outdoors plus a variety of other sports and fitness-oriented activities. However, Jim regularly catches nice fish by reaching spots others don't. He backpacks high into the Sierra, often with his wife Ruth, beyond where the average hiker goes, finding obscure lakes and streams.

He's not an equipment hound like some. Instead of shelling out cash for an item, he typically rigs his own version. He has glued outdoor carpeting to the bottom of sneaks to serve as wading shoes. For a float tube seat, Jim affixed a piece of carpeting with parachute cord on a large tire tube. I like to view his efforts as creative and environmentally responsible rather than parsimonious.

For our East Carson venture, we left the Bay Area mid-afternoon on a Friday, arriving four hours later at the base of the ridge. A quick hike up the hillside and down into the canyon brought us to the the river with little daylight left. Jim fished while I cooked dinner. He returned after having caught four good-sized fish, a fifteen-inch brown his best. I made a few casts myself without luck.

The next morning we put on our backpacks and proceeded downstream, heading for the hot springs. Fishing as we walked along the meandering river, we had to cross it back and forth many times. Hiking ahead of me, Jim picked up three fat rainbows. I caught nothing.

As we plodded on, across sandy and muddy shores, over slippery rocks in and along the river, Jim asked sometime in late afternoon, "Where the heck are these hot springs?" At this point we were three or four miles downriver. "They're up ahead," I said, realizing I should have checked a map beforehand. "We should be getting close."

As evening approached, we set up camp short of our destination, disappointed on missing out on a hot bath. Before dark, Jim hooked yet another nice trout. The best I could do was spot a couple of trout flash near my fly. With the elevation above 5000 feet, the September night was cold. A beautiful harvest moon glowed over us like a huge spotlight far into the night.

The next day we retraced our steps, again fishing all the way with backpacks on. We passed a dirt road used by four-wheelers to access the river. We saw the human contamination Ralph Cutter had alluded to: cans, bottles, gun shells, junk. There were signs of tire tracks that had ripped up sections of the fragile shoreline. Jim and I placed some of the litter in our packs to haul out.

Making our way upriver, I again couldn't get a trout to hit my fly with any commitment. Jim brought in a couple of more nice ones. So after two days of fishing, Jim had caught ten beauties while I got skunked. He didn't have the slightest idea what kind of fly worked best. "A bushy one" was all he could say. So much for fly fishing's finer points.

On the walk up the canyon side, we somehow got on the wrong ridge, causing us to hike two hours instead of one. True to character, Jim remained good-natured, easier when you're the one who caught all of the fish.

Evening Bites

It was time for Doug's annual fishing outing with me. We chose the East Carson.

Although not a zealous fisherman, Doug nevertheless is a rugged outdoorsman and gifted athlete. He likes to catch fish but tends to get bored if they aren't biting. Being more socially-oriented, he doesn't enjoy the solitude of the outdoors as much as Kirk and I do. When we do go fishing together, however, he is an enjoyable and sensitive companion, and I've always cherished our excursions together.

It was September and the East Carson was warm, low and clear. In the first run, Doug picked up a decent fish. Then the doldrums set in. I left Doug and headed downstream. At a long, promising pool, I put on a streamer fly. Making a short cast into a swirling mass of white water at the head of the pool, I intended to let the current carry the fly down the run. Within seconds, a large fish savagely struck my fly. Just as quickly the fish was off and I was left with a broken leader where a small knot used to be.

What the hell...? I wondered. I thought perhaps I had tied into a giant squaw fish or sucker—species known to inhabit the East Carson. The hit, however, didn't resemble a junk fish. Mumbling, I made my way back upriver, passing a fisherman whom I had leapfrogged over earlier.

"How's the fishing?" he asked. I told him about the mysterious monster that took my fly. "That was a brown," he said. "I was here last week and the same thing happened four times to me. The big browns are moving up from the reservoir. I have an eight-pound test leader today."

I moved on, now thoroughly ticked off knowing a trophy fish got away due to an equipment breakdown. When I reached

Doug, I told him my big-fish-that-got-away story, one he's heard many times before.

Doug and I fished our way back along the river, reaching one of my favorite pools with less than half an hour of daylight remaining. More than once, this long deep pool had rewarded me with a burst of fish activity just before dark.

The trout responded on schedule. A heavy fish jumped, followed by another. I saw a silver flash next to where I cast my fly. "Dad, we better get going," Doug said.

"I'm about to hook a good one," I said. "Just a couple more casts."

"There's not much light left."

"Yow, I've got one! Damn, missed it. Fifteen inches at least."

I made another cast. A fish zoomed out of the depths and hit the drifting caddis imitation. I struck back only to propel my unencumbered fly into a branch behind me. Cursing again, I retrieved the fly, losing precious minutes. I plowed back into the water up to my knees and sent out another long cast, letting the fly drift before twitching it across the pool A trout slashed at it. No hook-up. The fish just weren't engulfing the fly. I whipped the line off the water and shot it out again, and then again.

A stillness abruptly descended upon the pool. The flurry was over. With a sense of futility I reeled in. It's amazing how determined I can be trying to catch a fourteen-inch fish, only to immediately release it if successful.

The evening sky darkened as we hurried to the start of our route out. We disassembled our rods, replaced wet sneakers with hiking boots, and broke into our swiftest gait. "What's the record for hiking out of here?" Doug asked.

"Forty minutes," I said.

"I'm going to beat it," he said.

With his tremendous leg strength and youthful stamina, Doug forged ahead, quickly leaving me behind. I struggled just to maintain a steady pace over the loose rocks and gravel up the dry creek bed. Only the faintest traces of dusk remained.

Every once in a while, Doug called back to make sure I was following. After around twenty-five minutes, I could see the dim outline of the mountain ridge ahead. Doug had already reached the top. "I'm heading to the car," he yelled. "You okay?"

"I'll see ya there," I yelled back.

It was now pitch dark, but no problem, I thought. All I had to do was follow the creek bed until it ended and then pick my way to the ridge top. I figured I should reach the crest in another five to ten minutes.

Fighting darkness and the steep incline, I was forced to drop to my knees every so often to maintain stable contact with the mountain. After fifteen minutes or so, I still hadn't reached the ridge. In fact, I wasn't sure whether I was climbing up a grade.

Am I on level ground or an incline? I couldn't tell in the dark. I did know though that I was in a grove of tall trees, something that shouldn't have been there. Twenty minutes had passed since Doug disappeared. "Doug!" I yelled. No answer.

"Dougggg!" I yelled louder. Again, no response.

I was now walking with my arms extended in front of me to avoid hitting a tree. I couldn't see a damn thing. If there had been a cliff nearby, I would have walked right over it. I had no idea which direction I was heading.

Boy, this is really stupid, getting lost like this. I should have packed a flashlight. I tried to remain calm. I couldn't be too far off track.

Spending the night out here would be a real pain. I'm glad I'm not alone. Actually I am alone..."DOUGGGG!" I called as loudly as I could. No response.

"DOUGGGGGG!" Nothing.

Lost in the woods, enshrouded by darkness and silence, produced an unnerving, helpless feeling I had never experienced before. Reassuring myself once again that being lost was a temporary problem, I stopped to gather in my senses. I rotated slowly in a circle while peering into the blackness. In one direction I saw the faintest of glimmers—the last vestiges of light on the western horizon. The car was parked west of the mountain ridge. I headed that way, calling out every so often for Doug.

After one of my calls, I heard a faint reply far off in the distance, the nicest sound I had heard in a long time. I walked in that direction, every once in awhile calling and following Doug's reply for guidance. When finally I reached the car, Doug said, "What happened? I thought I was going to have to call in the bloodhounds."

I didn't have a good answer, being completely baffled on how I got so far off track in so short a time. Doug had indeed made a record ascent, reaching the car in thirty-five minutes. He had assumed I was following close behind.

We enjoyed a few more laughs about this episode as we drove back to our cabin. I kept to myself that, while I was walking in the woods lost and unable to see, I didn't laugh once. Not even a chuckle.

On a return trip to the East Carson the following year, I solved the cause of my screw-up. In an earlier visit, I had seen a fork in the creek bed near its top. The time when Jim and I had hiked far off to a different ridge, we had mistakenly followed the northwest branch of this fork. What I didn't note at the time was yet another obscure fork higher up the creek bed. In the dark I took the wrong branch of this second fork, sending me to the southeast and the forest of trees. So it is not enough to merely "follow the creek bed" out of the canyon. One has to be attentive and precise with landmarks—a task made even more difficult when one can't see.

River Musings

A year passed before I returned to the East Carson. This time I packed in my sleeping gear in order to be at the river for the prime evening fishing. I was not anxious to test my wilderness survival skills again by walking out in the dark.

Reaching the river in late morning, I left my gear in my camping spot and proceeded downriver. As I fished my favorite runs, it was clear the trout weren't interested in my offerings this clear September day. Nonetheless, I couldn't imagine being in a more tranquil setting.

After making a cast, I was startled by dirt and rocks sliding down a bank off to my right. A coyote emerged from the backside of a rock pinnacle, and then sat on the top, ten feet above the water. A shaft of sunlight imparted a golden hue to this handsome creature as it surveyed its domain, oblivious to my presence fifty feet away.

Toward midday I spotted an old aluminum chair at a camping spot and took a seat. The clear, crisp air, warm sun and gentle breezes soothed my body as I munched on a sandwich. After eating, I sat there, unwinding, listening to the river, reflecting.

Is being here, fly fishing, a good use of my time? Is it juvenile to be spending so much time in wild canyons?

I know I can't spend all of my time recreating. I also have to be doing things where I'm improving, learning, achieving progress of one sort or another. What kind of things? Completing a house project, improving an athletic skill, making a good investment return, planting trees and flowers, writing an article, reading a stimulating book, doing a good job in my work, growing in new ways.

I have a strong need to achieve, however not always in the conventional ways. I have always placed family and lifestyle ahead of career advancement. Time has been more important than money to me, although money can provide for leisure time. Having enough money so that it ceases to be very important in my life is what matters to me. Just so I don't spend too much time trying to make money...

I continued to sit, meditating, my mind roaming freely...

What are productive uses of time? Some persons spend most of their time pursuing job success, so-called workaholics. If they derive personal fulfillment from this choice, that's fine. When someone tells me they wish they could spend more time fly fishing but they don't have time, what they are really saying is they don't value this activity enough to make time to do it.

A person has to organize his time to match his values. If he devotes most of his energies to his career, or to making money, then that's where his values lie. That's all right, if that's what he really wants to do with his time.

Every person needs something where he finds inner peace. It may be through art, gardening, seminars, work, socializing, whatever. For me, it's fly fishing on a stream. To each his own, I say, just so long as he finds it.

A person may die in mid-life, like my friend Dick. Earlene said she wished they had done more things they had wanted to do. Now those opportunities are gone.

I need to focus on the present, and fully experience what's right in front of me, instead of always looking to a future payoff. Like the saying, "Wherever you go, there you are."

Many times when I'm doing something, even skiing, I get edgy, feeling as though things are waiting for me to do. What's waiting? When I'm fly fishing, I never have that feeling.

Am I contributing to my fellow man? I haven't been the volunteer type, but I've been involved in educating young people in my job. Most people work in business and may then contribute to their community in their spare time. Working in a public service job, as I have done, is community service. At least that's how I rationalize it.

Working on environmental issues is the way I try to make the world better. What's more important then preserving wilderness and all the creatures that inhabit the earth?

It all comes down to finding meaning in life—learning, growing, contributing to others, working to preserve the earth, devoting myself to family and friends. I need to spend my time doing things that I find meaningful and rewarding.

I used to be a church-going individual, and I still believe in the presence of a supreme being. Sometimes I think I need to be more outwardly religious again. But, being here is a spiritual experience for me. I feel as close to the important dimensions of life, as close to God, as I could be anywhere. Being here feels right, the elements present in this canyon seem meaningful, more meaningful than anything else. I feel at peace...

I could have sat in that chair all afternoon. But images of wild trout snapped me out of my reverie.

It was back to the serious business of fishing. As I plied the pools and runs with a nymph pattern, only an occasional trout flashed near my imitation. With the water low and clear, the trout swerved away quickly when detecting something unnatural. One trout came close and gave my fly a prolonged stare, allowing me to look directly into its eyes.

As evening approached, the trout became more active. I retraced my steps back upstream, and picked up at least one nice fish per pool. The action continued until dark. All told, I caught six rainbows above thirteen inches that evening.

I hiked out the canyon the next morning, thinking what fun it is to catch a robust trout on a fly in this beautiful place. It's as good a high as I need. I planned to return in a couple of weeks.

Never The Same Stream

On this return visit, the low, clear waters typical of the autumn made the trout cautious. Although I caught nothing all afternoon, I expected to catch my quota of "East Carson specials" come evening.

By mid-evening I was still fishless and had only two pools left before my hike out, not sleeping in the canyon this trip. When I approached the first pool, I saw trout rising to the surface as I hoped. I chose a #14 Elk Hair Caddis fly, a proven pattern for the East Carson, and cast, expecting a quick hit. Nothing. A large fish jumped a few feet away. I waited a few seconds and then cast my fly where it had jumped. No strike. Seeing small insects on the water's surface, I switched to a #16 pattern. I made my most delicate cast and allowed the fly to drift naturally to the feeding lane. Still nothing.

A fat trout porpoised to the surface a mere three feet from where I stood. The tail of another broke the water's surface. In both cases, their heads had been pointed downward, indicating they were taking nymphs rising to the surface.

I took off my dry fly, and tied on a Pheasant Tail nymph pattern. I sent the fly onto the current, allowed it to sink, and then lifted it to the surface to simulate the real thing. No hit. I repeated this maneuver several times without success. I hurriedly tried a short dropper line with a second nymph. Now I had two flies on my line, one to be fished deep, and one near the surface. Both flies were ignored.

After several more futile casts, I searched my fly box, looking for an emerger pattern. Perhaps these fish were taking the insect pupae in the surface film just as they were about to leave the water. I couldn't find an emerger fly in my box.

The fish swirled and slashed at something near the surface. I couldn't see any insects coming off the water. A small Royal Coachman fly has produced with East Carson trout in the past so I tried to tie one of these tiny flies onto my leader for several frustrating minutes in the dimming light. When I finally did, I made my cast. A trout jumped near my fly, teasing me into thinking it had struck my offering. It hadn't.

It was apparent I wasn't going to hook one of these fish. The trout were feeding on small nymphs or emergers near the surface and couldn't be fooled by my artificial presentations. I may have enticed a strike had I had an emerger pattern. Perhaps I failed to correctly duplicate the actions of the insects. With only about twenty minutes of light remaining, I left the pool with the trout still feeding, a fisherman's worst scenario.

I sloshed through the river to the trail, broke down my rod, put on my hiking shoes, and started hurrying up the hillside, concerned about getting caught in the dark again. Sweating furiously, I wheezed and gasped for breath as I pushed toward the ridge. My pounding heart told me I was in worse condition than I thought.

After reaching the top with a few minutes of light to spare, I then ambled to the car. On the ride home, I remained bugged by my failure to elicit a strike in the midst of a feeding frenzy, replaying in my mind what other tactics I might have used. I recalled that on my prior trip I had many hookups when there was no evidence of feeding fish, providing yet another example of the contrariness of wild trout. By the time I reached our cabin, I had digested the wisdom of the Greek philosopher Heraclitus who observed centuries ago that one never steps in the same stream twice.

The East Carson River has been good to me, but it's a fragile fishery. On the plus side, the trout can select from a smorgasbord of food sources, including prolific populations of insects, minnows, tadpoles, crayfish, snakes, bees, grasshoppers, beetles, ants and the like. The banks are marked by countless foot prints and droppings from a wide spectrum of birds and mammals that make this canyon such a tightly woven wildlife sanctuary.

The problems stem from all the usual sources: cows are allowed to graze the canyon thus degrading the water and surrounding environment; water from upper elevation tributaries is diverted to irrigate meadows, again for the benefit of cows; with the river running low in summer, silt builds up in the slower, deeper pools, causing me to have to clean the gills of a thrashing trout I brought to shore on occasion, not knowing if it would survive after I released it.

During low snowpack years, the East Carson's water level drops perilously low, and as summer progresses, the water temperature rises. The river resembles a small stream in sections, leaving the trout with few sections of decent holding water. A hard look needs to be given to upstream water diversions as the East Carson at present cannot support a strong population of wild trout, nor sustain a lot of fishing pressure. This conclusion has been verified by a recent count by the California Fish and Game Department indicating the river holds less than 400 fish per mile compared to other wild trout rivers that hold thousands of fish per mile.

Fortunately the East Carson has benefited from pro-preservation decisions and measures. The Watasheamu project—a long-standing proposal to dam the river, hence enriching the land speculators behind the project—was finally shown to be cost prohibitive and was laid to rest in 1981. The designations of the section below Hangman's Bridge as a "Wild Trout River" in 1984, and as a California "Wild and Scenic River" in 1989, have greatly helped protect the river and its wild trout. It is currently being considered for addition to the nation's wild and scenic river system, a designation that would greatly help to preserve the East Carson for future generations.

This unique river and its tranquil canyon have withstood man's assaults ever since silver was discovered in nearby

Nevada. The time has come for the East Carson to enjoy more than survival, to be allowed to become the complete wilderness river it is capable of being. The words of a Native American, Chief Seattle, the renowned Suquamish tribe leader for whom the city is named to honor the help he gave the first white settlers, say it best: "The rivers are our brothers. You must give to the rivers the kindness you would give your brothers."

Top, Kirk and dad on first Stanislaus raft trip
Above, Doug on the trail

The Mokelumne Wilderness

Top, Monte Wolf's cabin
Above, Doug on backpack trip to Mokelumne Wilderness

North Fork Mokelumne River

North Fork Stanislaus River

Fun times on the Stanislaus

Tuolumne River

First trip down the Tuolumne

Kirk brings in a Tuolumne trout

Rafting Tuolumne's Rock Garden

Author's Tuolumne camping companion
-a vital wilderness creature

East Carson River

Headwaters of the San Joaquin

The Lower San Joaquin-Middle Fork

Traces of early visitors to lower San Joaquin Canyon

Author on Mt. Whitney with wife Diane-the family's best hiker

7

New Territory: The San Joaquin

Who could ever guess that so rough a wilderness should yet be so fine, so full of good things. One seems to be in a majestic domed pavilion in which a grand play is being acted with scenery and music and incense.—**John Muir**

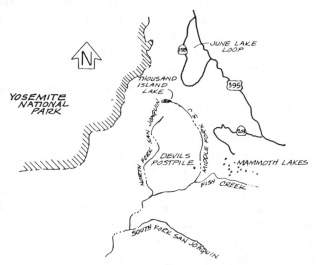

The Middle Fork of the San Joaquin begins where it flows out from Thousand Island Lake at 10,000 feet in the Ansel Adams Wilderness, south of Yosemite. From there it plummets down a long hanging canyon sitting at the base of the glacial-carved Minaret Range. The river gains volume from Shadow Creek which thunders down a series of spectacular drops before joining the San Joaquin. The river then flows past Agnews Meadows and on through Devils Postpile National Monument four miles further down. Two miles from the Monument's Visitor Center, the river drops dramatically over 140-foot Rainbow Falls.

Below the falls, the river flows through a rugged canyon on its way to the San Joaquin Valley and eventual rendezvous with the Sacramento River. The merger of these two rivers forms the huge tidal estuary known as the Sacramento-San Joaquin Delta which flows into the San Francisco Bay and eventually the Pacific Ocean. The San

Joaquin is California's longest river, it being 330 miles in length (three miles longer than the Sacramento), and the fifth largest in volume.

The name "San Joaquin" comes from the Spanish name for the revered father, Joachim, of the Virgin Mary. In 1813 a Spanish lieutenant named Marago discovered a small stream that headed in the high Sierra. He called it San Joaquin, a name subsequently given to the great Sierra river and the central valley where it flowed.

Miwok Indians from the central valley traveled along the San Joaquin to spend their summers in the mountains, and to trade with the Mono Indians from the eastern Sierra. For trade they carried acorns, shell beads, squaw berries, manzanita berries, elderberries, baskets, sea shells and a fungus used in paint.

The Monos ascended over Mammoth Pass and down to the lower San Joaquin where they met the Miwoks. For trading they brought obsidian for arrow and spear heads (a hill of large obsidian rocks is located off Highway 395 between the June Lake Loop and Mammoth Lakes), pine and pinyon nuts, pumice stone (another eastern Sierra product now used extensively to "wash" jeans), rabbit skin blankets, buffalo robes, salt, fly pupae from Mono Lake, and the larvae of the pandora moth.

Road builders hoped to construct a major trans-Sierra highway along the San Joaquin in the 1960s. This proposed "Minaret Summit Road" would have divided the longest road-free wilderness area in the lower forty-nine states. It did not receive approval. The passage of the California Wilderness Bill of 1984 established the Ansel Adams Wilderness Area in this region of the Inyo National Forest, ending any lingering developers' hopes for the summit road.

The visitor can drive to the San Joaquin River by going to the town of Mammoth Lakes in the eastern Sierra, continuing past the Mammoth Ski Area to Minaret Summit, and then down a steep road to the San Joaquin River and Devils Postpile National Monument. Several campgrounds are available here. The Western Divide is crossed at Minaret Summit thus producing a southwestern

114

flow to the San Joaquin through the heart of the Sierra Nevada, before heading north to join the Sacramento River.

A Stroll

While on a horse packing trip, I greeted the San Joaquin River for the first time at its headwaters flowing from Thousand Island Lake. My wife Diane and I became so enamored with the eastern Sierra, we started spending several weeks there each summer.

Along its spectacular run at the base of the Minarets, and on through one of the most rugged canyons in the Sierra, the Middle Fork of the San Joaquin is brimming with wild trout. On this exceptional trout stream, a fisherman can accomplish a fishing "grand slam": hooking a rainbow, brown, eastern brook and golden (hybrid) trout all in one day, sometimes even in the same pool. A determined angler can catch more than fifty fish a day, if he sets his mind and feet to it.

The San Joaquin, like most high-elevation rivers, lacks rich insect populations and consistent water volume to support a lot of big fish. So the wild trout are primarily small— averaging seven to ten inches. This is not to say that trout above ten inches on up to five pounds can't be caught. They can. But it is the ready availability of hungry trout and the beautiful surroundings that reward anglers.

Since my first visit to the San Joaquin, I explored new sections of it every summer. On the horse-pack trip, I fished the headwaters and the upper reaches. In years following, I hiked back there (as efficient as horse packing is, it chews up the land; walking is better), and also to the middle stretches, covering much of the water from Thousand Island Lake to Agnew Meadows near where the road first meets the river. I fished the four-mile section from the meadows to Devil's Postpile. I fished throughout the monument and below

Rainbow Falls, including far downstream in the narrow, boulder-strewn canyon. I figure if you're trying to become intimate with a river, you should leave few parts unexplored.

I even strolled to the Lower San Joaquin canyon, a region that sees few visitors in any given year. How I happened to find my way to this untrammeled region was not a simple matter.

One early August morning, Diane and I left June Lake for Devil's Postpile. She planned to hike while I fished—our usual routines. As we were driving past the Mammoth Ski Lodge, we saw an elderly hitchhiker standing in the parking lot with a mongrel dog and a huge red backpack sitting alongside him. Dressed in old garb, with a mountain climbing hat on, and various utensils and implements dangling from his pack, he looked like he was on his way to a mountain man rendezvous. I would have offered him a lift but our vehicle was full, plus Diane is appropriately wary of hitchhikers.

After dropping my wife off at the trailhead, I drove back toward Agnews Meadows where I planned to pick up the trail to the river. At the dirt road veering off into the meadow, I again saw the hitchhiker. He apparently had been given a ride down to this location and was looking for another.

I turned my truck around and motioned for him to climb aboard, figuring anyone who carried a huge backpack could be trusted. After placing his dog and pack in the back of my truck, he joined me in the cab. I took note of a large spinning rod ·attached to his pack.

"Name's Bob," I said shaking his hand.

"I'm Buck. The dog's Jake," he said. "Appreeciet the ride."

Jake was a brown and black mutt, perhaps a mix of collie and sheep dog. He appeared friendly but his eyes held a guarded look.

"Where're you heading?" I asked.

"To fish crick trailhead. Goin to ma camp in the lower San Joaquin," he said.

"Looks like you're planning on staying awhile," I said.

116

"Yep, ah'll be at this camp fer maybe four, five months. Then ah'll head out to ma winter camp on the lower Kern."

"How's the fishing down there?" I inquired.

"Waal, last year I got me two six-pound browns in less than ten minutes. Is that good enuff?"

He had my attention.

"Where's your camp?" I asked casually, not wanting to appear overly interested.

"The trail ain't on a map. Ya hav to go down fish crick trail. When it veers off and takes a steep turn east, after maybe seven, eight miles, ya go due west. When ya get to Pond Lily, ya'll hit the trail which takes you down to ma camp. Only way ta get there."

"Maybe I'll pay you a visit one of these days," I said as Buck was getting his pack and dog from the back of the truck.

"Now look here, you cum on down if ya can and ah'll show ya some great fishin," he said, hoisting his enormous pack to his back. He leashed Jake, and they started down the trail.

With images of big browns dancing in my head, I drove away knowing I was going to pay Buck a visit real soon. You don't run into six-pound browns every day. The notion of an individual living in the wild also intrigued me.

The next day Diane left for the Bay Area for a couple of days. I decided this was the time to visit Buck.

Early the following morning I headed to Devil's Postpile, purchasing a supreme roast beef deli sandwich to eat down in the canyon. Ordinarily I refrain from red meat, but I figured I needed extra fat and calories for this jaunt. In the café at Red's Meadow near the monument, I had a last cup of coffee before my hike.

At the trailhead I loaded my pack with my food (sandwich, granola bars, cheese and crackers, candy bars, muffins and fruit), drinks (water, orange juice and two cans of Bud), a chunk of ice in a sealed bag, and my fishing and sleeping gear. It was 8:30 when I started down the trail.

My main concern was locating the route to the lower San Joaquin, but that shouldn't be too difficult I thought. How hard could it be to find a river in a canyon? And if I didn't locate Buck's camp, I could still camp and fish.

The miles went by easily at first, through a lush forest of Red fir and Jeffrey pine. The trail then took me across the top of vertical granite walls, giving me grand vistas of the lower canyon. After what I estimated to be seven or eight miles, I started looking for that steep turn to the east Buck had mentioned. The trail did take several easterly turns but none seemed steep enough so I continued for another mile or so. When I came to a flat forested area bisected by a dry creek bed that veered to the right, I figured this was as good a place as any to head west.

I followed the creek bed through dense growth for a half mile before emerging onto open terrain where the gradient dropped more steeply. I picked my way down the waterless stream bed and, as I thought, arrived at the top of a canyon wall bisected by the rocky staircase I was following. Now all I had to do was negotiate my way down the staircase.

In lowering myself from one stone platform to the next, I descended much of the ravine. In some places, I had to grip a ledge while dropping down to the next, praying I would not meet an impasse further down. A hike back out this same route would have been a disaster at this point. Even worse in this remote location would have been an injury. *My lord, who would know where I was?* I pushed on with increased caution, not wanting to risk a stumble. With the sun beating down on me, sweat was pouring out of my body.

Although my pack was hefty, its interior frame design kept it well balanced and close to my body as I descended the gorge. I had bought this pack for exactly this kind of hiking. I only had another 150 feet or so before I hit the canyon bottom. After lowering myself to yet another platform, what I feared stood at my feet—a twelve-foot block of granite. I searched the front and sides of it for hand or foot holds enabling me to climb down but couldn't find any. A precarious maneuver here could be catastrophic. I stood there immobilized, the analytic

118

left side of my brain issuing a blaspheme at the creative right side.

When I turned and looked at the back of the granite block, I spotted a crevice. Inspecting it, I saw a passageway down to the bottom where there was an opening. I squeezed into the crevice, dropped down and emerged on the ledge below the granite block. *Whew...lucky move. Just keep moving now Robert.*

After a few more drops, there it was—a sparkling, emerald green, fast-flowing river. Sheer beauty! I completed the descent and stood at the river's bank, congratulating myself.

Looking around, I noted that the canyon walls on my side of the river were almost vertical. In a stroke of luck, I had chosen what seemed to be the only feasible way down. Now I was looking at one of the prettiest rivers I had ever seen. A check of my watch showed 12:30—four hours from when I started.

As I gazed at the river, something seemed wrong. *The river should be flowing the other way. What's going on here?* I pondered this puzzle for a moment, concluding this river was not the San Joaquin but rather Fish Creek, a major tributary. No problem I concluded, all I have to do is follow it to the San Joaquin. It occurred to me I should have brought a map.

I took a long drink from my water bottle, knowing now that I didn't bring enough water to get me through the trip. I wanted to gulp down volumes of the beautiful river water in front of me but the threat of contracting giardia deterred me. The left side of my brain again lashed out, this time at the stupidity of not bringing a water filter.

The cliffs blocked passage on my side of the river, but the other side offered walking room. Fortunately for me this was a low-water year so the river was not as full as it could have been—another break. With some difficulty I forded the stream, picked up a trail and proceeded downriver, all the time wondering how in the hell I was going to get home with those sheer rock walls on the other side staring at me. I concluded I would worry about that problem later.

At this point I was feeling pretty chipper. I had succeeded in getting to a beautiful place, a spectacular river was flowing at my feet, I was in no hurry to get somewhere. I rigged up my rod and started casting in the pools as I walked. On almost every cast, a wild rainbow tore into my fly. Although none exceeded eleven inches, they were good fighters.

After a mile, a twinge of concern crept into my head about not yet meeting the San Joaquin. I saw no side canyon up ahead where it might be flowing. It crossed my mind I could be lost. Hot, tired and thirsty, I trudged on. Even the fish had stopped biting. I was no longer feeling chipper.

I came to a section where the river canyon broadened to a forested basin. Huge fir, pine, cedar and oak trees gave this valley a tranquil, primeval appearance. I crossed the river with little idea where I was. After hiking steadily for the past five hours, all I could do was set up camp, get a good rest and figure out what to do in the morning.

Now totally weary I entered this inviting forest, intent only on plunking my body down and resting my aching legs. I walked about thirty yards and there, in front of me, was a bark-covered lean-to and a red backpack parked against a nearby tree—Buck's camp. My intuitive side had not let me down.

Dining Out

"Boy, am I happy to see you!" I said upon seeing Buck who jumped at the sound of my voice. Jake, also surprised, barked ferociously, but quickly settled down after recognizing me. He licked my hand and then placed his paws on my waist to sniff my backpack.

"Wal ah'll be. How the heck did ya get here?"

"I took a dry creek bed about a mile or so upriver. Don't know how I made it," I said. "I sure am happy to have found you...not sure how I was going to get back."

Buck turned around and pointed to a ridge. "See that notch up there? That's where the trail comes at. I still can't figure out how in tha dang ya got down here."

Behind Buck was a large lean-to made out of four- to five-inch diameter logs. It had sides, a sloping roof and an open front. On the top and sides, large strips of cedar bark covered a blue plastic tarp. A small radio sat on a rock, an aluminum chair was nearby, a bow saw hung on a limb, and various ropes, tarps and a magazine or two were strewn about.

A big, soot-blackened pot containing a simmering mix rested on a flat rock in the fireplace in front of the lean-to. Underneath the flat rock was a bed of glowing red coals encased on three sides by flat rocks, placed vertically, with small gaps between them for draft. The back rock jutted up above the others to reflect heat forward. The fireplace was close enough to the lean-to to project heat into it.

Happy to take my pack off, I leaned it against a tree and slumped to the ground exhausted. Buck offered a large cup of lemonade that I gratefully accepted. He said, "Don't ya worry about the water. Ah hav this big pot that ah boiled real good fer drinkin. Sheet, ah wouldn't touch that stuff in Fish Crick with all them people and animals camping above. Usually there's a cold spring water coming out uv them rocks back there, but it ain't runnin' this summer."

"I thought your camp was on the San Joaquin, not Fish Creek," I said.

"San Joaquin's a half mile down," Buck responded. "Ah set ma camp here whar the trail cums out. Ah'll take you ta the San Joaquin when ya want ta fish. How's about s'more lemonade?"

I gulped the rest of the warm liquid and handed him the cup for a refilling.

Buck told me he stayed here during the summer and fall, hiking to the town of Mammoth every few weeks for supplies, his social security check, and "a good Mexican or Chinese meal." He left this camp when it got cold, sometimes as late as December, often taking a couple of weeks to make it out through the snow. He then hitched rides to the Kern River in the southern Sierra where as he put it, "ah hav ma winter camp."

"Yep, ah liv in the best place around," Buck said, eyes gleaming. "Jus look around. This valley is as purty as Yosemite, and there ain't no people here."

Buck said he was born sixty-three years ago in Yosemite National Park where his father was a ranger. In past years he held odd jobs now and then, mainly at the Mammoth Ski Resort. He made an oblique reference to a blow on his head in the distant past which caused him trouble every so often. Other than this sketchy personal information, I couldn't get much more out of him.

I munched on snacks, drank more lemonade, and started to think of fishing. It was getting late in the afternoon. I pulled my vest out of my pack and assembled my rod.

Buck raised his backpack containing his food supplies over a tree limb high in the air via an elaborate hoist system. "There's bars here sometimes," he said. He took Jake off his rope and the mutt raced in a big circle, exuberantly free. Buck said he kept Jake leashed most of the time on account of rattlesnakes, not wanting to lose his sole companion.

Buck grabbed his huge spinning rod, a six-inch lure dangling from the end, and with Jake on a leash, motioned me to follow, saying he wanted to show me some Indian artifacts before we fished.

The first site he showed me was a large, flat-surfaced rock pockmarked with several deep holes used by Indians for grinding acorns. Some of the depressions were as deep as ten inches. Buck carefully scraped out debris from the holes so I could get a good photo.

He then took me to an unusual rock structure consisting of large rocks placed upright around a flat rock base to form a rectangle, sort of like an open rock tub. Buck surmised the structure was used in an Indian ceremony whereby a person sat in the enclosure with searing hot rocks placed on the outside of the structure. Branches were placed over the rocks, covering the person sitting in the tub. The hot rocks were then doused with water, creating a steam bath effect.

Convinced that a cache of weapons or other artifacts were hidden somewhere in the valley, Buck said he spent many hours combing the area. He claimed to have found one such cache in a different part of the Sierra that he turned over to a museum.

We moved on. Finally there was the elusive San Joaquin, crashing down from the north through an obscure, narrow canyon. "No way anyone cum down thet way," Buck said. "Okay now, ya fish on downstream frum here. Ah'll walk on down to one uv ma favorit holes whar the rivers meet. See ya there or back at camp."

The first few pools I tried were deep and separated by short waterfalls and cascades. After catching only one small rainbow in thirty minutes, I began to doubt Buck's claims. I then hit a tree-lined stretch where the river dropped in a succession of shelves, with pockets, ripples, glides and eddies throughout. With the river level down, I was able to rock jump, casting a dry fly to any part of the river.

The fish started hitting, often striking my fly within a split second after it touched the water. For the next two hours I lost all sense of weariness and time, being totally immersed in the melodic beat of the flowing stream, the propelling of the fly, and the responses of the wild creatures vibrating from my fly rod.

The trout were primarily fat, spirited rainbows in the ten-to twelve-inch range—real scrappy fighters. I picked up a few browns, keeping a fourteen incher to give Buck for dinner. No six pounders. They probably came upriver later in the season on their spawning runs, or perhaps were holding low in deeper holes.

When I reached the confluence of the two rivers about a half mile from where I started, Buck wasn't there. The river doubled in size here and I wished I had more time to explore runs downriver. But daylight was fading, and my weariness was beginning to register. I trudged back to camp, obsessed with thoughts of the cold beer and roast beef sandwich waiting for me.

Buck was cleaning a couple of small, seven-inch fish when I reached him. I wondered how he had caught such little guys with that big lure. I gave him my fourteen-inch brown which looked like a lunker next to his. Since Buck apparently kept all the fish he caught, I now knew why no fish were biting in Fish Creek near his camp—Buck had caught them all.

Watching him fry the fish in sizzling oil, I noted that his hands were as black as the fry pan. The mysterious concoction in his big pot still simmered and bubbled, looking grim. "How's about sum rice and bean stew?" he asked.

I politely declined, thinking why fill up on camp glop when I have a deli masterpiece to consume. I reached in my pack and hauled out my roast beef sandwich and a cold beer. I offered Buck the second can, hoping he wouldn't take it. He eyed it in a funny way before declining. Then on second thought, he let me pour a small amount into his cup from my can. "Fer later," he said. A strange reaction I thought.

I took a long swig of the cold beer, savoring every drop, then placed the can and my wrapped sandwich on a nearby rock. I went to my pack and dug out some crackers and cheese. When I returned to the rock, my roast beef dinner was gone. A short distance away, Jake was devouring it, the paper wrap in shreds. The cur had struck when I wasn't looking. Buck expressed the proper regrets and apologies. If he wasn't there, I would have used his hoist system to string Jake up the highest tree top.

Now I had no choice but to eat Buck's bean and rice stew. My second beer helped to make it more palatable. Famished as I was, the stew actually tasted pretty good. Buck insisted I have one of the fish which he handed to me in those black, now greasy, hands. Seasoned perfectly, it was delicious. Like a starved wolf, Jake consumed the heads, bones, tails and skin. The mongrel ate well this night.

After dinner Buck served hot chocolate. Out here in the wild, the sweet chocolate liquid tasted better than any dessert I have ever had. When it was time to turn in, Buck gave me an old sleeping bag to put under my air mattress for "sum extra paddin." He retired to his lean-to, I to a spot under the stars.

With bones aching and brain dulled from the beer, I crawled in my sleeping bag and quickly fell asleep. Opening my eyes hours later, I looked up to a black sky full of stars. A pungent pine aroma filled the crisp night air, resonating unceasingly with chirping insects and river melodies. I lay there completely enraptured, feeling pretty damn smug.

When daylight came and I crawled from my bag, Buck had a bowl of oatmeal waiting. I gave him a muffin, and also a candy bar that he eagerly placed in a food storage container. I washed breakfast down with orange juice and prepared for my hike out.

"How about stayin longer?" Buck asked. "Ah'll take you way downriver. The North Fork cums in six miles on down. Aw hav a camp there too. Real nice brookies there."

"Gotta go, Buck. My wife is coming back today and expects me at June Lake," I said.

"Come back later this summer," Buck said. "Stay awhile. Heck, we'll hike down the San Joaquin and yore wife can meet us on the west side whar a dirt road cums up and meets the river."

"Can't do it this summer, some other time maybe." I thought for a person choosing to live like a hermit, Buck sure liked my company. Plus he had been one of the most thoughtful and generous persons imaginable. Here's a man who packed in all his supplies, offering me some of everything he had. Perhaps he just appreciated that I came to see him. However I had to wonder about a person who retreats deep into the wilderness, away from human contact.

I tried to imagine what it must be like to live by yourself, camping twelve months a year in the woods. What would you do all day? There's only so much wood to chop, fish to catch, food to cook. From everything he said and did, Buck appeared genuine about his love for the outdoors and his lifestyle. But what lurked behind his choice of lifestyle?

There have always been individuals who drop out from society. Natty Bumpo and Huck Finn are two examples from the classics. I suspected from the way he spoke and few items he volunteered, that Buck didn't take well to conventional living. There's little doubt Buck was a misfit in today's world.

There are many homeless people in our country and I guess Buck would be counted among them. But unlike those looking for handouts, Buck takes responsibility for himself. Maybe camping year round was his best choice. I'd choose the wilderness over a park bench. But there are problems about this lifestyle. For one, it's illegal to camp more than two weeks in national forests. Second, what if many persons decided to set up camps in the mountains? Our public lands would be trashed. I guess the last place where one can actually live in the wilderness is a homestead in the Alaskan bush. In the lower forty eight, that choice no longer exists. Somebody forgot to tell Buck.

Buck and my friend Jake accompanied me to the trailhead for my hike out. He showed me the path and described the landmarks I needed to look for on the trek back. We shook hands and I was on my way.

The trip back was certainly easier than that of the previous day, although it seemed to take forever to reach Devil's Postpile. I felt "high" all the way back, and for many days thereafter. I had had one heck of an exhilarating adventure. It's not often a person finds such an enchanting, wild place where the trout and solitude are plentiful. I enjoyed my time with Buck. I could have done without Jake—at least his dining manners. I also knew I'd return to the lower San Joaquin again.

(Buck's Recipe for Bean and Rice Stew: Combine one pound of rice and large bag of dried beans in big pot of boiling water. Cook, keep simmering for days, adding water, oil, salt and pepper as needed. Flavor with whatever is handy: fish heads, bacon grease, rattlesnake meat. Eat anytime.)

The Wild Challenges

Later that summer after my visit to Buck, a major fire erupted in the forest below Rainbow Falls. First reported on August 20, it was presumed that lightning had ignited forest debris which smoldered a few days before bursting into flames. High winds and a parched forest from six years of drought produced an inferno, spreading wildly. Hikers and campers in the region were evacuated.

The rampage threatened structures in the Old Mammoth Lakes Basin region and the Mammoth Mountain Ski Resort. Residents and vacationers were ordered to leave. Meanwhile, the fire burned throughout the prime hiking country south of

Rainbow Falls—right where I had hiked just one month previous—and in the John Muir and Ansel Adams wilderness areas. In a desperate effort, volunteer firefighters saved the Red's Meadow Packing Resort.

Back in the Bay Area, hearing reports of "The Rainbow Fire," I thought of Buck and the region of his camp. I wondered about the fire's impact on the San Joaquin River and its fish.

Nine days after the fire had started, firefighters, including some from as far as Alaska, finally contained the blaze. It wasn't until late September, however, that the fire was fully controlled. By that time, over 9,000 acres of forest had been devastated.

The next summer Kirk, on a two-week leave from the Army, joined Diane and me at June Lake in early July. For a backpacking trip Kirk liked what I told him about the lower San Joaquin, agreeing it was the place to go. I expected to see Buck there.

Over the years, Kirk, who is as smitten on wild rivers and wilderness trout as I am, has been my most faithful fishing companion. When he was just a small tyke, he would lag way behind me as we tramped to those hard-to-get-to places in search of trout. In his mid-teens, still a small guy, he began leading the way. At the age of 26, he joined the U.S. Army, becoming a physical fitness zealot. By this time he had sprouted to his present 5'9," 150 lb. frame, and was soon winning fitness contests on his army bases. Now Kirk tackles the most challenging of hikes as though he's on a Sunday stroll. He is the most rugged outdoorsman I know, possessing not only endurance but also a tough-minded spirit. He'll sleep on the ground with barely a sleeping pad, often with no pillow. He'll fish long, empty hours without getting discouraged. He never complains or levels blame when one of my decisions backfires. He's just the greatest of outdoor companions.

On the Fish Creek Trail I knew we would be walking in the Rainbow Fire area, but I wasn't ready for what we saw. Where once stood a verdant forest, only charred tree trunks and stumps, gray dust and ashes, remained, looking like a lunar landscape. Hiking in the desolation, I couldn't help but think about forest fires and what they do or don't do. The massive fire in Yellowstone National Park in 1988 focused the issues. Aggressive fire suppression has long been the accepted forestry practice so whenever a fire raged out of control as happened in Yellowstone, like most persons I viewed it as a catastrophe. What was ignored is the critical role fire plays in the health of forest ecosystems. Some tree and plant species depend on fires for regeneration; fires thin various species of plants and trees, perpetuating the more adaptable species; smoke serves as a fumigant that controls the spread of forest diseases. Burned areas ultimately support more wildlife than non-burned areas since dense brush that discourages wildlife is replaced by sprouting shrubs and rich emergent grasses that herbivores thrive on, thus providing predators with more food.

There may be short-term consequences from forest fires while the ecosystem heals. Even though Mother Nature is tremendously resilient in repairing the earth, natural restorative processes make take decades or centuries, meaning an area may be drastically altered during one's lifetime. But such is the world of nature where centuries are infinitesimal increments of time.

Ironically, the suppression of fires actually increases fire danger and losses by allowing unnaturally large amounts of fuel to accumulate thereby insuring the next conflagration is intense and more destructive, as for example the Rainbow Fire. Such "crown fires" leave an almost sterile environment in their wake. Nonetheless a let-it-burn-approach is not without its downsides and critics. The threat fires pose to human dwellings and private properties cannot be ignored. Plus forest fire smoke, sometimes covering a wide area for weeks, creates pollution harmful to people. Not too surprisingly the timber industry argues it's better to remove dead and dying trees than to burn them. The practices that the Forest Service has recently adopted of treating fire as a friend rather than an enemy, and utilizing *controlled*, less intense burns, represent more ecologically-sound efforts. No responsible person supports fires that rage out of control.

What about the impact of fires on fisheries? Here too the findings are consoling. From the Yellowstone Fire we've learned that although there were some fish kills, the overall fishery in the park was not significantly harmed. The larger message was, if an ecosystem is healthy, so too will be the rivers and trout.

The devastation from the Rainbow Fire reminded me of a statement made on the Yellowstone Fire, that "wilderness, in order to remain wild, does shocking things." I thought this statement summed it up pretty well. Plus man's actions are by far the primary cause of environmental degradation. Fires pale by comparison.

After four miles Kirk and I left the barren landscape and found ourselves back in fresh Sierra greenery. The Rainbow Fire had not come close to the lower San Joaquin canyon. When it was near the distance to leave the Fish Creek Trail, I chose what I thought was the route to Buck's valley, and erred again. Kirk and I found ourselves on a steep mountain side. Sheer, impassable canyon walls dropped out of sight ahead.

We plowed through thick manzanita bushes, traversed across a wet, precipitous ravine, and then climbed back up a steep incline. This was as rugged terrain as I'd ever been in. With thoughts of deja vu, here I was huffing and sweating, looking for that bedeviling route to the lower San Joaquin. I was not a happy hiker. Meanwhile, Kirk motored up, down and across this inhospitable place like a mountain goat, with nary a complaint or a deep breath.

Back at the top of a ridge, we scanned the countryside and were able to get our bearings. We followed an animal path that luckily took us to Pond Lily and from there located the trail to the ridge and the path down to the valley floor. We had wasted two hours in aimless hiking.

When we reached Buck's camp he wasn't there. Strewn about were a tattered sleeping bag, broken aluminum chair, pots, cans, bottles, pieces of plastic tarp, and miscellaneous junk. The lean-to had collapsed; thousands of ants had invaded Buck's mattress and sleeping area. In my mind this mess was more unsightly than that caused by the Rainbow Fire.

I wondered if Buck had left in haste when the fire struck, fleeing to his lower camp downriver. Perhaps he wasn't even in this region at the time. The truth is, I didn't believe the fire had much to do with the mess here. I'm afraid Buck kept packing in stuff with no intention of ever hauling it out again. In addition to this mess, I wondered how many other "camps" Buck had left in similar shape. I also recalled how he ate wild trout all summer long, and how he burned large quantities of dead wood and branches. All it would take for this beautiful valley and its rivers to be ravaged would be to have a few more Bucks around. I felt betrayed.

I've seen other abandoned squatter "camps" that were blights on the land similar to Buck's. Anyone who establishes a camp out in the wild, especially for extended and repeated use, inflicts damage to the natural terrain. It's rare for an individual who abuses the land in this manner to then clean up the site. Thus we have sprinkled throughout our forests abandoned camps with fire pits filled with cans and tin foil, blackened rocks, cut logs, nails in trees, trampled ground, an absence of dead wood, and so forth.

The problems go far beyond squatter camps. Many people love going to the wilderness, often the most beautiful places, and have a rip snorting good time: four wheeling up and down hillsides, turning forest humus into dust; drinking heavily and blasting off rounds, using beer cans plus any other handy objects for target practice; chopping down trees for firewood and other human conveniences; then leaving cans, bottles, bullet casings, toilet paper and other debris behind when their "wilderness experience" is over. With this outlook—unfortunately dominant in the frontier mentality—wilderness exists to be used and conquered. And squatters and rednecks aren't the only modern day environmental desecrators. Backpackers contaminate the back country with cans and plastic tarps; fishermen clutter river banks with bait and lure

containers, messes of monofilament line, cans and their snap
openers. The list goes on and on.

"Let's pack out what we can on the way out," Kirk
suggested.

We hiked on, finding an ideal campsite near the
confluence of Fish Creek and the San Joaquin. This had been
an unusually wet year so the rivers were flowing high, making
the fishing difficult. But we managed to hook several good
trout along the edges of the rushing river.

With the fishing marginal we decided not to stay a second
night. The next morning we stopped at Buck's site, picked up
what we could carry, and then grunted up the side of the
canyon.

From the top of the ridge we proceeded to Pond Lily,
passing another pile of debris, this time the leftovers from a
bear feast on the supplies of a poor backpacker. Then we
mistakenly followed an animal trail that took us along a steep
mountainside once again. This area is not forgiving. Make one
mistake and you pay dearly. But it's magnificent in its
wildness. When we eventually found the true path, I
memorized some landmarks, intending not to lose my way in
this country ever again.

I have since thought about seeking help from an
environmental foundation to clean out Buck's camp. It would
take brute hiking to haul the junk to the top of the ridge, but
from there a couple of mules could carry the stuff out in no
time.

This remote valley, enclosed by vertical canyon walls, and
creased by rivers alive with wild trout, with its records of
native peoples, is sacred. A person should tread lightly and
leave no trace in such a place.

8
Fly Fishing Nuances

The fly fisherman is considered the most thoughtful artist on the river.— Les Hill & Graeme Marshall, <u>Stalking Trout</u>

I stood on a boulder alongside the Tuolumne and cast my fly to the other side of the long pool. The current took it down the run while I released more line to allow the longest drift possible. The fly was a black and white bivisible dry pattern, size ten. It represented no insect I'm aware of but I've had good success fishing attractor patterns in the heavy waters of the Tuolumne.

The evening light was fading. Since I had a mile walk back to my car, I only had another five minutes or so of fishing left. With no signs of feeding trout I figured I wasn't going to catch any fish this day.

I made another long cast. The current seized the fly, sending it on a long arc to the tail end of the pool where I left it skating back and forth. I waited for a strike but there was no sign of an interested trout. To my right I saw another good position upstream. I would make a cast or two from there before calling it a day.

With the rod cradled in the crook of my arm, the line and fly still in the water, I started to climb over a large granite boulder. As I scrambled on hands and knees, my back to the river, I felt a sudden jerk on my fly rod, accompanied by that familiar throbbing resistance. Before the rod was whipped out of my hands, I grabbed it and found myself playing a big trout that had managed to hook itself on a fly left dancing on the water while I maneuvered to get to a different position. The trout turned out to be one of my best hookups ever on the Tuolumne—a whopping eighteen-inch rainbow.

133

Troutspeak

Every field has its own vocabulary. Fly fishing is no different. Words and phrases provide the means to think about a given subject, which in turn affect actions. How and what we think about wild creatures determine how we treat or value them. For example, most outdoor activists understand that when people feed a wild creature, its behavior changes. The animal ceases to be "wild." The infamous bears of Yellowstone, begging for food along the park's highways, is a case in point. If people had treated these animals as wild they wouldn't have fed them, leaving the bears to forage for food as they've always done.

We can do better in defining "wild trout." Here's a concept driving much of the thinking about a healthy fishery, yet the narrow scope of its current definition restricts us from perhaps doing even more to protect the valued creatures that fall within its scope.

The widely accepted definition of a wild trout is *a free-living fish, hatched and reared in a stream, lake or sea from an egg spawned and deposited there by its mother*. This definition does not distinguish the most precious trout species that are native to their environments, i.e. *native trout*, from the other species of trout introduced to environments, e.g. brown trout, that often weaken or eliminate the native species. This distinction is being given more and more attention these days as people grasp the genetic uniqueness of these native creatures. But in addition, more related to the theme of this book, the current definition for a wild trout ignores *the impact of man on the behavior of the trout*—a factor that usually determines "wildness" in other creatures and places.

Consider trout in heavily-fished waters. Their holding lies are so bombarded with fishermen's offerings they may get hooked several times a season. Hot Creek in Mono County is such a river. A study conducted by the California Department of Fish and Game concluded: the *one mile* stretch of fishing water in one season supported 25,000 hours of fishing which

134

averages eleven fishermen on the creek every hour, seven days a week, dawn to dusk, May through October. Thirty thousand trout were caught and released with each fish hooked at least three or more times (not counting the number of near hook-ups where the trout escapes with a sore lip)! These fish are *free-living, wild* trout?? I would call them battered creatures that are trapped by hot springs upstream and downstream in a relationship from which they would love to flee.

Contrast Hot Creek trout with the trout I've been pursuing in hard-to-get-to places. Most of these latter fish have seldom if ever seen an artificial fly before. They live in a natural setting without man's intrusive presence. Clearly there is a world of difference between these trout and Hot Creek trout that calls for further distinctions on trout "wildness." The concept of "wilderness" can help here.

The federal *Wilderness Act of 1964* defines wilderness in part as "an area where the earth and its community of life are untrammeled by man..." With this definition, a trout could be considered a "wilderness" creature when its behavior is not impacted by man, or to put it more accurately, by man's use of a baited hook or artificial lure. A trout in waters never visited by man represents the rare case. Waters do exist, however, that harbor trout little influenced by man. They thrive in remote or hard-to-get-to places where "the imprint of man's work is substantially unnoticeable." (From *Wilderness Act.*) Surprisingly they can also be found in more accessible waters.

To the scholarly business of trout classifications, therefore, I am presenting a sub-category of wild trout that I call "wilderness trout," and define as "wild trout little impacted by man." This definition differentiates wilderness trout from those harried creatures in waters pounded by fishermen. The latter could be called "conditioned trout" to reflect that their behavior is being conditioned or shaped by man, albeit by aversive consequences, i.e. getting hooked.

Why is this exercise in nomenclature important? For the simple reason that, if our language helps us to determine what's most precious to preserve for future generations, then chances are we will do so. I can't think of anything more important to protect than wilderness trout and the places where they live.

Uncovering Wilderness Trout

Most fly fishing occurs on popular waters. The choice rivers in California—Hot Creek, Hat Creek, Fall River, East Walker, Upper and Lower Owens, Upper and Lower Sacramento— endure relentless pounding from fishermen. The same is true for blue ribbon trout waters in every other part of the country. For the angler who desires a quality fishing and outdoors experience in relative solitude, he must seek hard-to-get-to waters.

In prior chapters I've described steps I've taken to locate productive wilderness trout rivers and streams in California. Granted it does help to have mountains and canyons encompassing wild rivers in the region. But hard-to-get-to waters exist in many other states, even though it is becoming harder each year to find such places given the growing popularity of fly fishing. Even New Zealanders complain about helicopters transporting more and more anglers to remote waters that formerly saw few fishermen.

The most obvious places to find wilderness trout in the United States are in wilderness areas. One of the most significant pieces of conservation legislation ever produced by the U.S. Congress—The Wilderness Act of 1964—designated areas that provide protective shelters for wilderness trout waters. We should value to the fullest these special areas, and attempt to have more of them created.

Other wilderness trout spots can be found in "wild & scenic" rivers, waters in national parks and U.S. forests, and in other untrammeled lands. And although I did not emphasize them in my own personal explorations, hundreds of thousands of lakes, with few visitors and bountiful stores of wilderness trout, occupy our nation's mountain ranges and wooded areas.

Besides these obvious sanctuaries, any hard-to-get-to waters holding trout may reward the adventurer. Find them, search them out. Part of the payoff here is the joy of taking the less traveled pathways and uncovering hidden sanctuaries.

136

To locate water harboring wilderness trout doesn't always require a long hike to a remote river. Even easily accessible waterways and heavily fished rivers often contain sections ignored by most fishermen due to one obstacle or another. The trick is to find a section of river not easily accessed, that requires scrambling down a steep bank or around a rocky embankment, or aggressive wading. Through such tactics, the angler can present a fly in water that 99.9% of other fishermen bypass, and uncover fish that seldomly see an artificial fly or lure.

Here's one example. In late October one year, I fished the North Fork of the Feather River where it enters Lake Almanor in Northern California. Large browns from the lake migrate up this stream on their fall spawning runs, only to encounter a gauntlet of fishermen—mainly locals armed with nightcrawlers—anxious to hook one of these lunkers. On this day, after attempts to spot fish up and down the river, and hundreds of casts, all without success, I concluded the spawning season was past and the river empty of fish.

While walking back along the river, I came to a bend where the current had thrust a huge mass of branches and uprooted saplings against the bank. At the rear of this brush pile, I looked down and saw a large fish tail in the water among the sunken limbs. I dropped to my knees to peer into the debris and saw several more tails, and then the backs of more than a dozen large browns. The entangled mass of branches prevented me from sinking a fly down to where the current was bringing food to these trout that had found a refuge, albeit a temporary one, from the bait of anglers. It is this kind of spot on a popular river, albeit one more capable of accepting a fly, that the determined angler attempts to find. (I do have to admit that the trout in the above example are being influenced by the presence of humans. It's just that they have managed to outsmart the angling hordes for the time being.)

What Turns Them On?

Fly fishing literature is replete with documented evidence,

anecdotal reports, and sage advice on effective strategies for hooking trout. I will confine my observations here to a few factors that I have found particularly useful when fly fishing for wilderness trout.

The concept of **selectivity** offers insight into the behavior of trout. It is usually defined as a trout's adherence to a particular diet. Some waterways are rich in insect and aquatic life. The trout in these waters, including wilderness trout in some cases, grow accustomed to one or more food types and are less willing to indulge in new ones. A variation of this same theme occurs when trout feed only on the insects most prevalent in or on the water at that given time, or just one stage of the insect's development, such as during an insect hatch. The trout in these cases are "selective" feeders.

Other waters, including many mountain rivers, present less rich and consistent sources of food so the trout have to be more opportunistic feeders. Any morsel of food is potentially attractive. These fish are not selective and will often strike readily at any fly offering.

Trout selectivity is also related to their contact with humans. The more a trout is hooked, and released, or almost hooked, the more selective and conditioned the trout becomes. As someone once said to me, "you're training fish to be smarter." The experienced angler knows that, when fishing for conditioned trout, selectivity can take more than one form. One of the plusses of wilderness trout angling is that the trout are not conditioned by human intrusions and hence not selective on this basis.

What about **fly patterns**? The standard maxim of "matching the hatch" applies when wilderness trout are keyed into a distinct source of food. In such cases, the fly fisher better identify what the trout are feeding on, and how they are taking their food, and then choose his fly and make his presentation accordingly.

When waters holding wilderness trout don't have consistent insect hatches, fly selection isn't so particular. Two strategies for accommodating the trout's opportunistic feeding needs are: 1) use a fly that represents a food type that the trout are familiar with; 2) use a fly not representing any specific life form but which attracts the trout.

For the former strategy, terrestrial patterns (e.g. grasshoppers, beetles, ants, bees, worms, caterpillars) represent standard food sources for trout. Add to these a few dry fly patterns (e.g. Elk Hair Caddis, Adams) to simulate insects common to rivers, nymph patterns (e.g. Birds Nest, Gold Ribbed Hares Ear) to simulate underwater insect life, and streamer patterns (e.g. Wooly Bugger, Muddler Minnow) to simulate minnows, and the fisherman is well equipped to fish for wilderness trout.

The second strategy is to use a fly that attracts the trout and dupes it into striking due to its hunger, curiosity, anger or any other reason known only to the trout. Standard attractor surface patterns (e.g. Royal Coachman, Royal Wulff, Royal Trude, Sierra Bright Dot, Renegade), and underwater patterns (e.g. wooly worm flies of varied sizes and colors) complete an assortment of flies targeted for non-selective, wilderness trout.

The informed angler today knows the importance of **water temperature** and the tendency of trout to feed when the water temperature reaches a certain point. The optimum temperature range for trout to become active on most waters is from 58 to 64 degrees, and the experienced fisher knows that fishing will be most productive when the water temperature falls within this range.

Depending on location and time of the year, some waters may never reach this optimum range. In November the water may stay below 58 degrees. Or in August the water may never get down to 64 degrees. During these days, however, the water temperature will change and offer a window of opportunity for the fisherman. During a cold time of year, the window may be between 1 p.m. and 3 p.m. when the sun warms up the water a degree or two. Conversely, during hot weather the productive times will likely be the early morning or evening hours when the water is cooler. A fisherman can use a water thermometer to detect those times when a shift is occurring and improve his odds of encountering active fish. (If nothing else, knowing the temperature of the water gives the angler more reasons to cite on why he didn't catch anything, e.g. "water was too cold today.")

Of all the factors that account for fishing success, the most important is the fisherman's ability to identify where trout are most likely to be holding and feeding. i.e., **good holding water**. This ability is closely related to the whitewater boatsman's ability to "read water"—knowledge typically acquired through study and experience.

Ralph Cutter in his well-researched book, *Sierra Trout Guide*, writes, "THE most important element of a trout water is oxygen content... At temperatures above 64 degrees trout go into a survival mode where they must seek water of richer oxygen content."

In summer when the days are hot and the water warms up, trout move from the slow moving pools where oxygen supplies are low to more oxygenated tumbling, rushing and churning water. During these months the experienced angler will seek out this kind of water. For example, on my first fishing trip to the Mokelumne, I plied the long, slow runs with my bait and didn't see any evidence of trout. My two sons meanwhile were pulling in fish right and left in a stretch of gushing rapids where the trout had collected during the hot summer days.

Regardless of the physical conditions and the feeding activity, or lack of feeding activity, of trout at any given moment, fly fishermen are successful in direct proportion to their knowledge and ability. A commonly accepted belief is that a small percentage (ten percent) of anglers catch most (ninety percent) of the fish. My experiences support this conclusion. I've seen anglers who don't make connections with trout while another person, under the same conditions, does. So how does someone improve his fly fishing skills and get up there with the ten percenters?

In addition to all of the accumulated wisdom presented by the masters in response to this question, I would emphasize one skill particularly effective for wilderness trout—the fly fisher's ability to entice and provoke a trout to hit a fly *through imparting action to the fly*, in contrast to the more orthodox method of utilizing a dead-drift or natural-drift approach.

140

As is true for other wild creatures within a natural environment, where the principle of survival of the fittest reigns, fish are predatory and cannibalistic creatures. When a wild trout sees a bug or minnow in a vulnerable position, it is likely to take a whack at it. How often have you seen a moth or grasshopper land on the surface of a stream and start thrashing about? Ninety-nine per cent of the time, if there is a trout lurking nearby, it will pluck that creature off the water's surface. The thrashing attracts the trout and signals a vulnerable or escaping prey, thus arousing the trout's predatory instincts. The fly fisherman would do well to duplicate such action with an artificial fly—a skill not easy to accomplish.

More times than I care to admit, I have caught some of my best fish each season when I have left my fly in the water to be tugged about by the current while my attention was elsewhere (see the anecdote at the beginning of this chapter), or as I was quitting and reeling in my line. I recall one such experience on the Firehole River in Yellowstone. Just before dark I was casting a big dry fly to rising trout near the opposite bank with no success. Before launching one final cast, I whipped the fly back across the water along the near bank in a hasty retrieve. A nineteen-inch brown savagely hit the fly. In fishing as in life, sometimes the best things happen when you're not trying so hard to achieve a particular result.

On countless occasions I have dead-drifted a nymph through a run without eliciting a strike. When I pulled the nymph across the run to simulate a fleeing insect or minnow, I was usually able to coax a trout out of hiding, either to inspect the streaking object, seize it in its mouth, or knock it without necessarily engorging it. The effectiveness of this tactic also tells me I should be using streamer patterns more since it's obvious big fish like to eat smaller fish.

Similarly, on a few memorable occasions, I have hooked a trout as I was lifting my fly out of the water, after having teased it back and forth in the current for a while without eliciting a strike. There's something about a prey swimming to get away, or just about to exit the scene, that triggers a response from the trout similar to that of other predators. For instance if you are confronted by a grizzly bear or mountain lion, the prevailing recommendation is that you hold your ground. If you turn and run the bear or lion is more likely to give chase. Another explanation for a trout's response may be that of something becoming more desirable as it is about to get away.

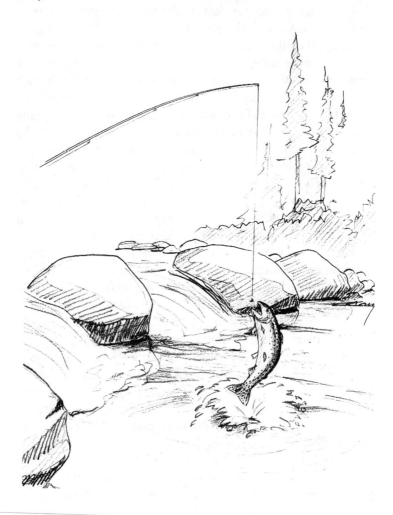

Imparting action to a fly produces results. The objective is to provoke or seduce the trout into striking. Barry Thornton's tactic in New Zealand was to cast his nymph hard and fast right at the trout's snout. Even when Barry was fully visible to the trout, its immediate reaction was to hit the fly.

So in answer to the query of how an angler moves into the select ten percent of fishermen who experience ninety percent of the hookups, i.e. the elite class, I offer the following when fishing for wilderness trout:

The angler should execute the standard tactics as recommended by the masters, including the selection of a fly pattern that represents the insect(s) the trout are feeding on at that time, and the presentation of his fly in a natural manner so as to simulate the specific behavior of the insect.

If this natural presentation doesn't produce any strikes, then the elite fly fisherman plays to the instincts of his quarry by seeking to entice, provoke, seduce, tease, anger, challenge, tempt or cajole the trout. He brings life to his dry fly by causing it to dance, skate, twitch, skitter, bounce, scurry, jitterbug or dart.

When trout are holding deep, the angler will simulate the life forms within the water's depths by causing a streamer or nymph pattern to drift, rise, dart and dash so as to arouse a trout's predatory instincts.

The elite angler will discover and utilize all of the craftsman-like and artful things he can do with a rod, line and fly that entice and provoke a trout to strike his fly offering.

When all of the above tactics fail, the successful angler will still get and keep his fly in the water as much as possible, because when all is said and done, it's the only way to catch fish.

The Rippling Of Rivers

When I'm fly fishing, I am fully immersed in the present, seldomly thinking of anything else. The tying on of a fly, the casting, the watching of a drifting fly or line, the timing and precision required to hook a fish—these are all mind-absorbing and relaxing activities. There's something intoxicating about casting an artificial fly and having a trout, regardless of size, come up and strike it, or sip it, jump at it, slash at it. I experience few greater "highs" than when a good-sized trout hits my fly and I successfully set the hook.

When I used to play tennis, I was in a constant state of turbulence and frustration. Errors usually determine who wins or loses a tennis match. When I would make the same error game after game, even though I "knew" how the stroke should be executed, my stomach became a mangled mash of knots. Losing was gut-wrenching. I typically left the court feeling highly aroused and ill-tempered rather than tranquil and relaxed, not to mention all of the damage produced on my body (e.g. sore back, shoulder tears, tennis elbow, tendonitis in the wrist). One would hope to derive more positive benefits from a sport. But then again, that was me and how I played the game.

I feel no such frustration and inner turbulence when fly fishing. I do make errors which occasionally cause me to lose a fish, but they do not deflate me, too much. I do cuss from time to time when my leader breaks (again) when I'm bringing in a good fish, or when I hook a branch or weed behind me. But most of the time, I am calm and relaxed when fly fishing.

I find something even more mentally refreshing about this endeavor, and that is the essential simplicity of it. True, one can study and improve in the tactical nuances of the sport for decades—a feature I find highly motivating. The differences between a novice and an elite fly fisherman are legion. But when I arrive at a river, and begin casting a fly, I am focused strictly on whether I can entice a trout to strike the fly. I have found nothing more mind healing than this simple quest. There is power in simplicity.

Some fishermen don't need to catch fish to feel successful, an approach similar to taking a hike where the process itself provides the reward. I can relate to this outlook. After all, being in the outdoors, communing with nature, getting exercise—these are all stimulating activities. Why measure success by the number or size of trout hooked? Well I have to admit I don't possess that outlook, although I admire it in others.

I enjoy fly fishing more, much more, when I'm hooking trout. When I do have a good outing, which can mean little more than one above-average-sized fish hooked and landed, and then released, my spirits and morale soar. I feel that life is good and worthwhile, and that my efforts have been validated.

When I don't catch fish, I feel unfulfilled. I become more intent upon finding new ways and places to catch wild trout. This is not to disparage the singular pleasure I take in going to the outdoors. It's just that having wild trout participate with me in the experience by showing some interest in my presence makes it a whole lot better.

So hooking a trout on a fly is important to me. One reason is that I am completely enamored with the beauty of trout. Ever since I saw my first trout a long time ago in Connecticut, I have remained mesmerized by the physical magnificence of this fish species: the smooth lines, vibrant coloring, combinations of spots and streaks, the iridescent shimmering. When I bring one of these creatures to shore, I always take in its beauty before I release it.

Besides the beauty of wild trout, I am enraptured with wild streams and rivers. Norman Maclean concluded his classic book, *A River Runs Through It,* with the words, "I am haunted by waters." Well I am transfixed by streams and rivers. When I am at a river, whether immersed in it so the current presses against my legs, or in a raft being pulled along effortlessly downriver, or resting alongside listening to the river's rhythmic song, I feel the pulse of the earth. The constancy of flowing water seems to reflect the flow of life itself. When I return to a river, I feel as though I am returning to where I should be.

Over the years I have expended tremendous energy to get to water holding wild trout. In my early years, I considered such efforts necessary but irksome. But with each passing year, I have grown to value the way there. The arduousness of the

145

trip becomes a measure of my personal well being. I can feel my body and spirit growing in toughness.

In order to get to places where I leave behind most other fishermen, and find the solitude I value, I must make a commitment. The more I push myself, the more obstacles I overcome, the more pleasure I gain. Why? Because of what I find and experience: solitude, a personal connection with the natural world, an opportunity to fish untrammeled waters for trout that are truly wild, a spiritual refurbishment, a chance to observe the rich biodiversity of river canyons unimpacted by man, a sense of being part of a natural system wherein all things are linked across time and place.

There is still more. The flow of water in a wilderness setting communicates to me something beyond physical phenomenon. I relax and feel more at peace than anywhere else where I spend time, similar to Henry David Thoreau who wrote, "who hears the rippling of rivers will not utterly despair of anything." The unity of nature is there, felt. A spiritual presence? Most assuredly. Persons find this presence in many different ways and places. Some people never find it. I recently read where a rock climber said she felt "close to God when rock climbing." I feel this force, this unifying power, when I am on a river.

The preservation of wilderness and wild creatures is vital to the well being of ourselves and our world. Why is this so? There are many eloquent spokespersons who have presented answers to this question, including Thoreau once again who wrote, "In wildness is the preservation of the world." I can only say that I find such places vital to me, to my health and well being, to my mental and spiritual needs. I have to go to these places on a regular basis, not only to be challenged by spirited trout in a wild river setting, but to nourish my spiritual life. When I am in a wilderness, I know that I am where the action is, where the most important elements of life are present.

9
Preparing For Wilderness

Something will have gone out of us as a people if we ever let the remaining wilderness be destroyed.—Wallace Stegner, <u>The Meaning of Wilderness in American Civilization</u>

Kirk and I were fishing in one our favorite stretches in the Mokelumne Wilderness. We planned to hike out of the canyon later in the day. With sweat pouring out of my body this hot August afternoon, I just couldn't get enough to drink. I had already consumed all of the water we had boiled that morning. We couldn't risk drinking from the Mokelumne River because of the threat of giardia. My mouth felt like cotton.

We crossed a small stream flowing down the hillside. Figuring its water was safer than that of the river, we quenched our thirsts from it. We then filled our water bottles and walked back to where our backpacks lay waiting.

Our route was straight up an escarpment gouged out of the steep side of the canyon by a massive avalanche. The top of the reddish dirt landslip looked miles away, and yet it accounted for less than half the distance to where our car was parked. I sucked in my stomach and started the ascent.

After thirty minutes, I had consumed half of the water in my quart bottle, craving water to a degree I had never experienced before. All of the water lost from sweating—probably gallons—needed to be replenished. Kirk as usual broke out into a strong gait up the grade, soon leaving me far behind.

I plodded on step by painful step with one image in mind—the cold beer waiting for me in the ice chest in the car. *If I could only have it now!* I tried to ration my remaining water but couldn't stop myself from drinking. Before I had gone a third of the way up the avalanche, my water bottle was empty, my mouth screaming for liquid.

As I forced my legs to move uphill, mumbling to myself as though delirious, I saw water flowing down the hillside in an orange-colored, slimy trough. It had a rusty-looking residue that I had seen many times in stagnant water. What did it signify? Minerals? Iron deposits? Polluted matter?

When I peered closely, the water's surface looked clear. I placed my bottle so that it skimmed water from the top until it was filled. Some items were suspended in the liquid but no rust-colored matter. I gulped the warm water until the bottle was empty. I refilled the bottle and drank another half a quart. I then filled the bottle to the top again. With a bloated stomach, I resumed my march up the hill.

Never before had I grasped the supreme role of water in sustaining life as I had on that hike out of the Mokelumne Wilderness.

Being Prepared

Any wilderness activity involves risks. To avoid putting life and limb in harm's way, the wilderness trout angler must possess outdoors knowledge and skills.

To avoid dehydration, an adequate supply of drinking water is vital. Carry enough water if on a day trip. For overnights, or extensive day outings, bring a water filter to insure safe drinking. Several of the models on the market are small and compact, and relatively inexpensive. Bringing water to a boil is the safest method for purification. Iodine tablets also rid the water of some protozoans such as *giardia lamblia,* but they are ineffective against another—c*ryptosporidium*—a newer contaminant with similar symptoms to giardia. Both are spread through animal feces so especially avoid those water sources below where mammals—either wild or domesticated—hang out. Since human waste also spreads giardia, never drink downstream from a camping area. If absolutely necessary, it's less risky to drink from a small side stream or spring.

The ravages of poison oak can be avoided or reduced by wearing long-sleeved shirts and long pants. Always rinse in the nearest waterway as soon as possible after being near poison oak. Creams for protective applications *before* you come in contact with poison oak, and for application *afterwards*, are available in drug stores. Note that poison oak is far less virulent in late summer and the fall when the leaves have dried than it is in spring and early summer when the leaves are shiny.

The outdoorsman should carry a first-aid kit containing the tapes, bandages, ointments, medicines, and other paraphernalia as recommended in outdoor journals. In addition, bring along a waterproof container of matches (could be a regular matchpack in a small zip-lock plastic bag), a compact space blanket which is little more than a durable sheet of silver foil, an extractor for insect, bee or snake bites, and a Swiss army knife or facsimile. For those bothersome blisters, moleskin is invaluable. A cheap substitute is duct tape, capable of fulfilling many other purposes as well. The foremost consideration is to be prepared for any contingency.

A turn in the weather is always possible. A non-bulky sheet of plastic for use as a cover is easy to pack and will protect you from getting drenched. Always carry a wool or polyester shirt on an extended trip as either material can keep you warm even if it gets wet. Cotton is often worse when wet than nothing at all as it takes warmth away from your body and keeps you chilled. If cold storms are a possibility, then you need to bring additional clothing: wind breaker, rain jacket, gloves, change of socks, warm hat, and so forth. Adding and subtracting layers of clothing is the best approach for dealing with weather, and the serious danger of hypothermia.

Getting lost, or worse, getting injured in a remote location can be a serious problem. When hiking in unfamiliar country, it's essential to carry a good map of that area. For the extreme adventurer who explores wild country under any and all conditions, it is advisable to possess a compass, altimeter and map-orienteering knowledge. A close relative or friend should always know where you are going to initiate a search in case

149

you don't return when you say you will. Hiking with a companion is a good practice for adventuresome trips. A cellular phone may also prove helpful.

The wilderness trout angler is going to wear different clothes than the conventional fly fisher. Waders and felt-soled wading shoes won't be necessary; in fact, they will be a downright hindrance as well as dangerous to wear around wild rivers. Instead, wear light, durable clothing and footwear. I typically wear long pants and a long sleeved shirt to safeguard my body from briars, poison oak, ticks and other hazards while hiking. When I fish, I usually wear nylon sports pants under a pair of hiking shorts; they protect my legs, and dry quickly if they get wet.

For footwear I look for sneaks or boots that have good soles for traction on slippery rocks. Vibram soles found on many hiking boots are the worst; on wet rocks they are like ice skates. The best material is probably rubber. The stealth rubber soles used in rock climbing shoes can now be found on hiking and wading shoes and provide excellent traction. I prefer inexpensive shoes that are durable enough for short hikes, e.g. two to three miles, and which I don't mind getting wet. My best finds have come from military surplus stores. To slip on around camp, I bring along a pair of light shoes, either running sneaks or water slippers, perhaps both. For longer hikes, I wear a good pair of hiking boots, replaced by my river shoes once I hit the river.

You should carry a flashlight for those times you get caught hiking in the dark. Many varieties of small but powerful flashlights are available.

In sum, when you spend time on a wild river, you want clothing and footwear that enable you to maneuver freely along the rugged shoreline while also protecting you from cuts, scratches and bites. Add a well-stocked fishing vest, a wide-brimmed hat for sun, the aforementioned items for safety and comfort, and you're all set to fish in wilderness trout country.

Lightning

One outdoor hazard meriting special attention is lightning. Lightning strikes the earth more than 8.6 million times each day with approximately twenty million lightning bolts striking ground in the United States each year. More people have been killed by lightning in this country in the past forty years—an average of 163 deaths a year—than by any other weather-related phenomenon. The odds of a person being struck by lightning are approximately 1 in 600,000 just based on statistical probability. If you're outside during a lightning storm, the odds dramatically increase.

To minimize the risks from lightning, here is what experts advise:

- Try not to be outside if a lightning storm is a possibility. If you are outdoors when a lightning storm approaches, take cover well before its onset as lightning can strike up to ten miles before the arrival of the actual storm.
- Stay away from mountain summits, exposed ridges, tall trees or open meadows, and a single standing tree in the open. A canoe on the water is extremely vulnerable.
- Avoid caves since a lightning strike can electrify the walls of the cave.
- If you're caught in a storm, seek out a stand of trees of roughly equal size in a low area; avoid standing in or near water, and on tree trunks and roots.
- If you're caught in the open, crouch down on the balls of your feet and become as much like a ball yourself as possible; place an insulating material under your feet such as a sleeping bag, or foam sleeping pad; try not to place your hands on the ground.
- Don't huddle together with other persons; lightning can pass from one body to the other.
- Don't set up your tent where a struck limb can come crashing down on it and you.

- Stay away from metals that will conduct electrical waves such as tent and backpack frames, fishing rods, etc.; place such items out of reach but nearby so that if lightning strikes, it will be attracted more to those items than to you.
- Do not leave your cover until the storm has fully passed; more people are killed both before and after the peak of the storm when they mistakenly think they are safe.
- Know CPR; immediate treatment for a stricken companion can save his or her life.

The best precaution with respect to lightning is to avoid the circumstances that place you in a vulnerable position.

Creatures Of The Wild

It's rare for a backpacker, fisherman, hunter or hiker to see a poisonous snake, let alone get bitten by one. If bitten, the chance of dying is less than two per cent, much less for a strong, healthy adult or when medical treatment is readily available. (The young and the infirm are most vulnerable to the dangers of a snake bite so particular precautions should be taken to prevent a child or sickly individual from being bitten. Dogs too are vulnerable.) Twenty or less fatalities from snakebite are typically recorded in the United States per year (compared to the 163 deaths caused by lightning). So we're not talking about a danger that should intimidate a person from spending time in the wilds. But poisonous snakes are found in all lower forty-eight states, with rattlesnakes being the most numerous. And they are dangerous, so their presence merits attention.

Ironically, more rattlesnake bites occur in familiar places, such as near one's home or in the nearby vicinity, than out in the wild. Common activities leading to rattlesnake bites have included: picking berries or flowers, gardening, gathering firewood (including in home wood piles), working in fields or roadsides, clearing brush, drinking from a spring, walking at

152

night (rattlers like the stored warmth of roadways), and stepping out from a car.

While fishing along rivers and streams, I try to keep the presence of rattlesnakes uppermost in my consciousness, and not make a stupid mistake like putting my hand in some place I can't see. Despite my vigilance, most of my rattlesnake meetings have surprised me, encountering snakes in places and at times I least expected.

Contrary to popular opinion, rattlesnakes can be found as high as 10,000 feet, even higher in warm climates. They might be up and about when the outside temperature is between 60 and 100 degrees F, but even this range should not be fully trusted. They seek opportunities to be in their optimal *bodily temperature* range—between 80 and 90 degrees F—in a number of ways such as being on a warm road at night, or in a cool, shady spot during hot weather.

Rattlesnakes are primarily nocturnal, especially when the days are hot. Not surprisingly, their prey (e.g. small rodents) are also predominantly nocturnal, which makes sense—for the rattlesnake. Even though I have never encountered a rattlesnake at night, at least not to my knowledge, I've learned to be even more cautious when daylight disappears. I would hate to step on a rattler in the dark, especially one of the monsters I've seen.

With few exceptions, the rattlesnakes I've come across have either remained still in hopes of going unnoticed, or have quickly retreated to safety. The only aggressive behavior I've witnessed occurred when the creature was caught in a vulnerable position. And even then, the snake didn't attempt to strike, only to warn. On those regrettable occasions when I have killed a rattlesnake, each one was doing its best to keep the peace.

However, not all rattlesnakes can be counted on to behave the same. Some are more apt to be aggressive than others, depending on time of the year, circumstances under which they are encountered, individual temperament, and the type of rattlesnake. So it would be a mistake to believe that every rattlesnake will remain still, beat a path to safety, or issue a warning. Every rattlesnake should be regarded as dangerous.

According to Laurence M. Klauber, a researcher who was recognized as the leading authority on rattlesnakes before his death in 1968, the majority of cases involving a person bitten by a rattlesnake fall into two categories: 1) Either a person puts his hands or other parts of his body into a place where a rattler lies concealed; or 2) A person is preoccupied with another activity so that he ceases to be alert to the possible presence of a rattlesnake. Klauber's advice: look where you put your hands and feet; don't put them in places without looking, and don't put them in places where you can't look.

What should you do if you are bitten? The list of "don'ts" looks like this:
1. Do not panic and get frantic; such a high state of excitement makes the effects of a bite worse.
2. Do not apply oral suction to the bite.
3. Do not cut or make incisions near the bite; the potential dangers from doing this are apt to be worse than the bite.
4. Do not apply a tourniquet; the dangers, e.g. onset of gangrene, of this procedure can be severe.
5. Do not attempt to freeze the wound or apply ice or cold packs.
6. Do not drink any alcohol.

Here is the list of "do's:"
1. Do apply suction to the wound if you can do so within five minutes of the bite (commercial suction devices— "extractors"—are available).
2. Do allow the bitten area to bleed freely.
3. Do clean area thoroughly.
4. Do apply direct pressure over the bite area; place a gauze pad on the bite area and wrap with an Ace bandage.
5. Immobilize bitten extremity; use a splint if necessary.
6. Keep bitten extremity below the heart; you might place a not-too-tight constriction band between the bite and your heart to slow down the movement of venom to your circulatory system.

7. Get to a medical office or hospital as soon as possible, but without getting your bodily functions racing.

The problem of being bitten far away from medical attention, in places where the pursuer of wilderness trout typically finds himself, is not a good one. The person in such an unenviable position should know that rattlesnakes do not always discharge venom when they bite. Swelling, discoloration and pain are indicators that venom has been discharged.

Given the paucity of effective first aid procedures that can be applied out in the wild, let's summarize again the best course to follow by citing two crucial rules: Rule 1. Don't ever get careless or inattentive and put yourself in a position to get bitten. Rule 2. ALWAYS follow rule 1.

Other hazards are out there in the wild, but far less risky than those encountered daily in and around communities and highways. The presence of bears (I'm talking about black bears here, not grizzlies) constitutes a hazard of sorts, more to your food supplies than to your body. Take the necessary precautions by stringing food up and out of reach of any marauding bears. Recent advice says you should shout, bang a pot, and generally not allow the bear to intimidate you on his way to what he may think is an easy meal. However, don't challenge or aggravate the bear in any way, nor get close to a mother bear with a cub. (I did once in an attempt to get a good photo. The shot I got off was of the ground during my very hasty retreat with the bear in hot pursuit.)

The other mammal meriting attention is the mountain lion. It has now doubled in population in California to 6,000 in the past decade as a result of a hunting ban. Mountain lion sightings have become more frequent, and three human deaths in the Golden State since 1994 have been attributed to these large cats—the first such deaths in eighty years.

The hiker/fisherman needs to be aware of mountain lions. These daunting and beautiful creatures are most apt to be active in the early morning or evening hours. They usually

155

attack a creature from its blind side, aiming at the victim's neck. It is highly unlikely for a mountain lion to attack a human, especially a medium to large individual, but one just might. Extra precautions should be taken with children and pets.

If you do confront a mountain lion, the recommended behavior is *not* to turn your back and run but to stand tall and firm, while trying to look as large as possible by raising your arms, backpack, or whatever is handy. Speaking loudly while slowly backing away may also help to dissuade the potential attacker. I'm more concerned about the lion I don't see, especially since I frequently walk by overhanging cliffs in the dusk. The danger is a minute one to be sure. But the knowledgeable outdoorsman should be aware of all possible dangers out there, and know where he is at all times. Carrying a stout hiking stick is a good idea.

Going to the wilderness does carry with it some risk. However, all of the elements which make up the habitat of wilderness trout—the wild creatures, rough terrain, weather, untamed rivers—are also the elements that make these places so special.

10
Preserving Wild Trout

A thing is right when it tends to preserve the integrity, stability, and beauty of the biotic community. It is wrong when it tends otherwise.—**Aldo Leopold, A Sand County Almanac.**

I wedged my wading staff down against the bottom of the East Walker River, the strong current pushing against my thighs. Large, slippery rocks obstructed my route to the run I intended to fish in this rapid-filled stretch. I've enjoyed fair-to-good success with a short-line nymphing technique in this kind of swirling pocket water.

Fishing was slow on this hot, sunny day. I only hooked three small browns in four hours. Here in mid-August, the river was running higher than usual causing me to wonder why so much water was released from the reservoir in the middle of a drought.

An unexpected surge of water plowed into me as I stood in the middle of the river, almost knocking me down. I leaned on my staff and headed back to the shore with as much speed as I could muster. Standing on the bank, I observed the river's flow. Sure enough, the water level was rising. But why?

Several weeks later, a brief newspaper piece reported a massive fish kill had occurred on the East Walker, caused by the draining of Bridgeport Reservoir by the Walker River Irrigation District of Nevada (WRID). When the reservoir was drained, precipitating the high flows I experienced, a massive plume of silt had accompanied the surge of high water. The District, apparently anticipating a shortage of water with the drought, had seized the moment to capture as much water as possible in its own reservoir far downstream in Nevada. In the process, the silt flushed down the channel of this blue ribbon trout river had choked off the oxygen supply of thousands of fish.

157

It's The Habitat

American river systems are in a state of peril. The national organization, *American Rivers*, states: "Today, at least 80 to 90 percent of riparian habitat in most western states has been eliminated by development and urbanization." The remaining habitat is threatened by further development. In its seminal study entitled *Restoration of Aquatic Ecosystems*, released in 1992, the National Research Council of the National Academy of Sciences urged a new national priority be given to the restoration and protection of the nation's rivers.

A 1993 report sponsored by the State Lands Commission of California, entitled, "California Rivers: A Public Trust Report," painted a similarly depressing picture of rivers in California. The report clearly demonstrated the health of California's rivers to be stressed and their viability as sustainable ecosystems to be in peril. It further stated that "it should no longer be disputed that there exists an urgent need for state agencies to undertake a comprehensive program of river basin and watershed protection and restoration."

Many factors contribute to the deterioration of river systems and water quality that imperil the well-being of wild trout. These factors can take place over time as in the case of Norman Maclean's beloved Blackfoot River (the river in his book, *A River Runs Through It*) in Montana. The Blackfoot's demise occurred from decades of abuse, primarily the loss of riparian habitat produced by logging. Eventually the river's trout couldn't be sustained in water where silt covered the spawning beds and where loss of riparian vegetation caused an increase in water temperature. Current human efforts and Nature's healing powers have been slowly repairing the damage to the Blackfoot and restoring the fishery.

A river's deterioration can also be immediate and catastrophic as with the East Walker (described above) in September, 1988, and the Upper Sacramento in July, 1991— two of California's blue ribbon trout rivers. The story of the Upper Sacramento has been well told. On a July day in 1991, a rail car turned over while the train was making a turn on the

158

track alongside the river. The deadly chemical in the car—metam sodium—was dumped into the river and carried downriver from Dunsmuir to Lake Shasta, killing every living organism in a forty-mile stretch. The river's rehabilitation, including the restoration of foliage and food chains to support the wild trout population, is taking years. (In the case of the East Walker, a court determined that the Walker River Irrigation District did not have autonomy over water releases from the Bridgeport Resevoir, and that adequate flows have to be maintained to protect the fishery. The river successfully came back as a rich fishery.)

In the space of three years, two of California's richest wild trout rivers were ruined. The abrupt circumstances that produced these catastrophes should alert us all to the fragile nature of our waterways.

Wild trout require healthy river systems and bodies of water to survive. The necessary conditions include: sufficient quantities of clean water year round to sustain the fish population, adequate food supplies, sufficient oxygen content, an acceptable temperature range, and places where trout can rest and hide. To these natural factors should be added protection from destructive human influences, such as development, degradation of habitat, and overharvesting of the fish population.

Following is a summary of the most harmful threats to rivers and river habitats:

Grazing. The Sierra Club has identified grazing as the primary cause of fishery degradation in the West. Grazing eradicates native plant species, and destroys delicate riverine systems. Cattle chisel and trample stream banks, widening channels, increasing erosion, warming waters and contaminating them with fecal matter. Grazing has permanently damaged many Sierra meadows.

Dams and Diversions. Dams starve rivers of oxygen and cause highly fluctuating temperatures and flows—all destructive to plant life and fisheries. Dams trap sediment and food that otherwise flow downstream. They block the movement of migratory and anadromous fish such as salmon, steelhead, and sea-run trout. Diversions (e.g. aqueducts, irrigation channels, recreational uses) rob streams and rivers of their full supply of water, often with disastrous ecological results.

Agriculture. Farming practices are the number one source of pollutants (e.g. sediment, animal waste, nutrients, pesticides) in waterways. Toxic substances in herbicides and pesticides that are absorbed on soil particles enter streams from soil leaching. Agriculture alters river-riparian ecosystems.

Flood Control and Channelization. Channelization causes the loss of habitat diversity created by bends, pool/riffle sequences, sunken woody debris and other irregularities. It destroys riparian habitat and eliminates the shading and food production provided by overhanging vegetation to the detriment of the aquatic community.

Exhaust and Chemical Emissions. Pollutants from farm chemicals and exhaust emissions, both auto and industrial, produce smog that is carried to forests and mountains, harming flora and fauna. Acidification occurs when nitrous oxides and sulfur dioxides from emissions are transformed into nitric and sulfuric acids, forming acid rain and snow that damage trees, water quality and fisheries.

Mining. Aggregate mining (the largest mining industry in California) alters stream beds and destroys river habitats. Toxic substances from mines spill into streams and rivers. Pollutants are leached from the ores into the waterways. Suction-dredge gold mining "vacuums" the bottoms of rivers with destructive results to their ecology.

Timber Harvest. Timber production and logging roads alter watersheds by increasing runoff and delivery of fine sediment to stream channels, decreasing summer flows, increasing upland erosion and altering natural drainage patterns. As a result, riparian habitat is damaged or destroyed, adversely affecting water quality and increasing its temperature.

Urbanization. Urbanization places structures in the path of natural processes. Deposits from the urbanscape, including trace metals such as cadmium, copper, lead and zinc, vehicular gasoline and oil residues, find their way into waterways through runoff and drainage systems.

Recreation. Trash and litter pollute river environments. Sewage from marinas is often disposed of directly into the rivers, an illegal action not effectively enforced. Fueling accidents, leaky tanks and lines, and carelessness allow spilled oil, diesel, gasoline, paint and toxic chemicals to enter rivers. Two-stroke engines on motor boats and personal watercrafts discharge quantities of contaminants into the water.

Riverside Development. Development destroys riparian habitat. Flood control measures result in further vegetation removal. Today, even with at least 80-90 percent of riparian habitat in most western states eliminated, the remaining pieces are still being threatened by development. Development in flood plains creates a need for dams and levees that destroy fish and wildlife habitat while placing more people and property at risk.

Spotted Owls, Old Growth Forests, and Wild Trout

For its sustenance, a healthy river system—from headwaters to the ocean—needs to be part of a healthy ecosystem: the interlocking relationships among the land forms, surrounding forests and riparian vegetation, vertebrate animals, aquatic habitats and food supplies. Given the crucial importance of ecosystems, and of individual plant and animal species, I went searching for a good, clean example of species interdependence, and clear answers to some of the questions I keep hearing in places such as lumber yards. Like, who needs spotted owls? Or, why should a worthless toad or snail prevent a building from being constructed? Since many of these issues are being addressed in the political arena, environmentalists need to respond to such questions in ways all citizens can understand. (Fly fishers and other environmentally conscious anglers also need to answer the charges that we "elitists" want to restrict fishing in all of the good waters to single, barbless hooks, and catch and release only; that is, just for ourselves.)

I discovered there are no simple answers to these questions; clear examples of species interdependence are hard to come by. But, and this is a huge but, *the more that scientists learn about ecosystems and biological diversity—the full, natural array of species and all the processes associated with them—the more vital they are seen to mankind and the earth.* It is apparent that Nature offers more answers and secrets than we yet know how to access. As the Jewish Philosopher, Mainmonides, wrote in the Twelfth Century, "In the realm of Nature, there is nothing purposeless, trivial or unnecessary." Now, how does one go about explaining this truth?

The first axiom to establish is the essential value of diversity—not as easy to prove in the world of nature as it is say in economic matters. Nonetheless, the more varied and complex a culture, the greater stability it possesses, and the more adaptable it is to change. When the inevitable changes do occur, such a culture is more apt to survive than one less varied and complex, and hence more subject to catastrophic losses. Translation: maintaining biological diversity throughout the world is paramount; it's too risky to eradicate any single species since its elimination may trigger the demise of other species, thus leading to simpler and simpler cultures. Since we really don't know everything about the functioning of biological communities, the only prudent course is to trust the wisdom of Nature and ecosystems.

Another aspect of biological diversity is the genetic diversity *within species.* If trout and salmon represent the Salmonidae fish family, then a rainbow trout represents a species within this family. But there are different subspecies of rainbow trout that have evolved in particular drainages, e.g. the Kern River rainbow trout. Such subspecies exist throughout nature, unique specimens with their own gene pools developed over eons of time in adaptation to their environments. If one of these subspecies is extirpated, or combined with another subspecies so as to become hybridized, the subspecies and its

162

unique genetic composition are forever gone. Only in the last few decades have fish biologists been able to report unequivocally that a healthy fishery depends on maintaining the genetic diversity among subspecies of fish families. Hybridization weakens fish families.

Man-produced changes to ecosystems, whether intentional or not, sometimes wreak havoc on the natural system. Exotic plants seize the land from native ones; an introduced species with no natural enemies, e.g. African snails, rabbits, multiply beyond control, causing severe damage to the environment. Feral pigs in Great Smoky National Park, mules in the Grand Canyon, wild mustangs in Nevada, are examples of introduced species producing untold damage to the native environments. The introduction of lake trout in Yellowstone Lake threatens the native cutthroat trout fishery in the lake, and also the bears, osprey, eagles and otters that consume the cutthroat. On the other hand, the introduction of trout to New Zealand's waters has been viewed as a successful adaptation, at least from the standpoint of benefits to humans.

The effects on ecosystems from the loss of certain species referred to as "apex" or "keystone" predator species are often readily observable. When one of these predator species, e.g. wolves, mountain lions, sharks, are reduced or eliminated, the numbers of their prey often skyrocket, causing the carefully balanced ecosystem to go haywire. Such keystone species are said to exert "top-down control" in ecosystems.

Something more subtle and long term, but nevertheless of grave importance, is how predators influence the development of other species. Without any predators many New Zealand birds, including the country's namesake—the Kiwi—evolved to be flightless. Would trout still be the wild creatures we cherish in the absence of osprey, eagles, herons, otters, and pelicans?

Less easy to grasp about ecosystems is "bottom-up control." Here, lower elements in the system are the primary reason the system functions as it does. For example, water that flows over chalk and limestone formations has higher concentrations of alkalinity and other nutrients usually correlated with fish abundance. Such "hard" water also contains more carbon dioxide than "soft" water which promotes the growth of algae through increased photosynthesis. The resulting proliferation of algae is then consumed by insects, either directly through grazing or indirectly through the collection of the loose remains of dead algae cells (detritus). Increased abundance and diversity of insects promotes increased quantities of fish that in turn sustains fish-eating creatures. An ecosystem develops that is rich in biotic diversity and resilient to changes and upheavals.

Examples of high alkaline waters that support a rich trout fishery are the chalk streams in England, and the limestone streams in Pennsylvania. Closer to my home, Eagle Lake in northern California is famous for its unique sub-species of rainbow trout that thrives in the high alkaline waters of the lake. Hot Creek in the eastern Sierra also contains higher alkaline and nutrient content than most waters due to its thermal origins, presenting rich algae, insect and trout populations. It's also true that excessively high alkaline waters will be largely devoid of plant or fish life, e.g. Mono Lake in the eastern Sierra.

Now where does this leave us with regard to those question on species interdependence? In the case of the spotted owl, the controversies have focused on a single species which is far too limited a field of vision and hence opens the door to uninformed critics. Full attention should be given to the owl *and its habitat—old growth forests.*

Old growth forests (there are also complex forest structures without old growth trees but which nevertheless possess similar characteristics to old growth forests) give and preserve life by creating soil, preventing erosion, producing oxygen, and removing carbon dioxide and various pollutants from the atmosphere. Their rich soils produce nutrients critical for sustaining diverse plant life. Some bird species build their nests in the high, dense canopies of old growth trees and nowhere else. Mammal species thrive in these forests, but will not do so in immature forests or in clear-cut sections. Clean water accumulates in the greenery, is stored in the soil, and is released slowly, minimizing flooding and drought.

Old growth forests sustain healthy streams and rivers, and their wild trout and salmon. Meanwhile, forests that have been widely logged produce heavy run-off which in turn sends dirt and silt into the waterways, destroying fish habitat. Logging removes tree canopies, increasing water temperatures and harming cold water fisheries.

Despite their immeasurable value, *only ten per cent of the former acreage of old growth forests is still standing in the United States.* The tree farms that now exist where old growth forests and complex forests once stood represent impoverished monocultures, incapable of sustaining the biological diversity which the earth so desperately requires, and capable of collapsing altogether.

What constitutes an old growth forest? Different numerical definitions exist depending on tree species, moisture regime, density of the tree canopy, the amount of nutrients on the ground, nesting trees, presence of snags and debris, as well as other factors. Most foresters and biologists agree that for a forested ecosystem to be healthy, old-growth stands should compose at least ten percent of its whole.

How old is an "old growth" tree? It depends on the species. Some bristlecone pines in the Inyo Mountains on the eastern Sierra are *over 4,000 years old,* thus standing 2,000 years before Christ! The giant sequoia trees in the Sierra have reached ages of 3,000 years.

Because spotted owls live primarily in old growth forests (in the Sierra their habitat can also be complex forest structures that do not necessarily contain old growth trees), their decline mirrors a decline in these rich, complex ecosystems, largely unprotected in past logging practices. Such a species is called an "indicator" or "flagship" species" whose very status manifests the health of their habitats. The spotted owl further serves as an "umbrella" for other wildlife. (Another indicator species closer to the realm of angling is the coho salmon; its declining status closely reflects the poor health of the many waterways across the Northwest where they previously flourished. May flies and stone flies are also indicator species for the health of waters.)

After having identified spotted owls as an indicator species for the health of old growth forests, I presented this rationale for their importance to a close friend, a biology major. He read it over and then asked, "but *why is the spotted owl the indicator?* Why not the trees themselves? What makes spotted owls so special?" Realizing there still must be missing pieces in the case for the spotted owl, I pursued his questions further and came up the following:

- The documented decline of the spotted owl is what led scientists to see that the owls' habitat was in decline—a complex issue of grave importance.

- The spotted owl (as is true for birds generally) is sensitive to habitat changes, and therefore in contrast to the trees themselves, allows for short-term changes to be identified. It serves as a primary test on whether the protection of old growth forests is actually working.

- Birds of prey such as the spotted owl (and eagles, hawks, falcons, ospreys, vultures), occupy the same position in the food chain as humans. If these raptor species disappear, one can assume that there are bigger underlying problems such as the presence of chemicals and pesticides in the environment, thus providing a forewarning on the health of humans.

- The loss of the spotted owl would deprive the world of the genetic uniqueness of this raptor species, leading to decreased genetic variability throughout nature (this same argument of course holds for any individual species).

- The accommodating ways of the spotted owl, e.g. its comfort with humans, has permitted thorough studies on its decline, producing comprehensive data on an endangered species.

- Laws exist to protect the spotted owl; they are less available to protect trees. The spotted owl has become the surrogate or guardian for the protection of forests.

So why are spotted owls of critical importance? Because the little remaining acreage of old growth and complex forests in this country, with their intricate network of life forms, and their ability to nurture environmental health, is of critical importance to wildlife and humankind. As one colleague said, it's less a matter of humans protecting the spotted owl than it is one where the spotted owl is protecting forests, and hence mankind.

Once the basic principles underlying ecosystems are understood, filling in the pieces on how all of this affects wild trout grows easier, for the future of wild trout is inextricably linked to the health of the other plant and animal species throughout the ecosystem. The well-being of wild trout depends on the preservation and, in many cases restoration, of complex river habitats.

Waterways need to be set aside and maintained as regulated wild trout fisheries, protected from man's varied assaults.

Wild trout need to be insulated from hatchery-reared fish that threaten their survival. When hatchery-reared fish are introduced into waters, they upset the natural functioning of the aquatic community, and will often interbreed with the wild trout, weakening the latter's genetic makeup. If this pattern continues, all of our waterways will eventually be populated by genetically weak, mongrelized trout.

We have to preserve those native species of trout possessing the unique genetic makeup evolved over centuries, from introduced species where this is still possible, and from hatchery-reared fish that threaten their survival. Already some native trout species have been rendered extinct or close to extinct because of these developments.

Preserving wild trout requires an understanding of ecosystems and biological diversity, and the political will to carry out what they are telling us.

The How of Preserving Wild Trout.

The ongoing degradation of American rivers and wilderness trout habitat, and declines in old growth forests and biodiversity, portend the continuing decline of wild trout. Anti-regulation and pro-development groups such as the "wise use" and "property rights" coalitions are vigorously seeking to overturn existing environmental safeguards, with particular aim at the Endangered Species Act (see Appendix for description of this act). Polls indicate the majority of Americans want the environment protected but special interests influence, some would say dictate, political outcomes. Conservationists must be intensely active in the public arena if the health of American rivers is to be safeguarded, and improved. You can play an instrumental role in this effort by:

- Becoming informed and involved on issues relating to wilderness trout and wilderness habitat.
- Learning about specific rivers that you fish, the issues affecting them, and becoming an advocate for their protection.
- Creating public awareness and support for your waters.
- Informing persons, newspapers and agencies on the ways your fishing activities support the local economy and community.
- Publicizing and documenting your involvement with rivers and wild trout through articles, photographs, slide shows, talks, etc.
- Praising and acknowledging the positive efforts of editors, politicians and other key officials when they take steps to protect the environment.
- Joining those organizations dedicated to wilderness and river preservation (e.g. *Friends of the River, Sierra Club, Nature Conservancy, Wilderness Society, Audubon Society, American Rivers*, local river coalitions).

- Becoming members of organizations dedicated to preserving wild trout (e.g. *CalTrout, Trout Unlimited.*)
- Volunteering in efforts to improve and preserve wilderness trout habitat.
- Being active politically through letters, phone calls, volunteering, voting and monetary contributions.
- Informing politicians of your personal interest and involvement in specific rivers and other environmental issues.
- Writing letters to your local newspaper; politicians do pay attention to newspaper items that mention their names.
- Supporting political candidates who are pro-environment.
- Being an environmentally responsible individual.
- Improving your own health and that of our fragile lands by consuming less red meat.
- Practicing catch and release.
- Recognizing that being called an "elitist" because you want to preserve our environment by inflicting as little damage on it as possible is a badge of honor, to be worn with pride. The earth needs as many elitists as possible.

Wilderness Values

The concept "wilderness" has not mixed well with the American character, which has been molded more thoroughly by America's "frontier" experience. Throughout our history, wilderness has been something to conquer, use, clear, mine, makeover, plow up, possess, dredge, inundate, fence in, pave, and develop. Native wilderness creatures have been slaughtered and dispossessed of their natural habitats. These represent the values of the frontier. Yet Americans, acting through their elected representatives, have had the wisdom to preserve selected wilderness areas, and wild rivers, and as a result, have discovered their contributions to the human spirit and to the integrity of the American civilization.

What are wilderness values? Recounting my own experiences in pursuing wild trout, as I have done in this book, has led me to ponder how I have changed as a result of my own wilderness experiences, and about ways that wilderness contributes to the well-being of humankind and our earth. On the basis of these reflections, I offer the following as wilderness values.

All life forms are deemed purposeful and vital. In wilderness each creature has meaning. Each species, with its unique genetic makeup and function, is allowed to exist and evolve naturally. Highest priority is given to maintaining the earth's biological diversity.

The interdependence of species is recognized and protected. Our planet's health depends upon the unimpeded functioning of the evolutionary process, sustaining the interlocking web of life. Wilderness provides an optimum environment for this principle to operate.

Commitment is made to the preservation of wilderness. Priority must be given to preserving the natural environment: the air, waterways, oceans, land forms, creatures and flora, instead of destroying or interfering with wilderness to suit selfish purposes and materialistic gain. A wilderness ethic causes an individual to leave a natural setting undisturbed, and even in a more natural state than as he found it.

Priority is given to natural processes. The essential wisdom and truths inherent in natural evolutionary processes supersede our human ability to choose what should or should not exist, or how nature should function. The wildness of nature is to be accepted on its own terms. Man's manipulations of the natural world, e.g. introducing species foreign to an ecosystem, need to be restricted, and in some cases, reversed.

Humankind's connections with the natural world are recognized and enhanced. Wilderness fosters inner peace, mental and emotional health, and spiritual connections with the natural world, critical to the health of all people and our planet.

171

Humankind's intrinsic love of nature needs to be respected and cultivated.

A commitment is given to community. Wilderness promotes togetherness, and a spirit of working together for the common good. A community consists of interdependent linkages among all its members, including humans as one citizen within the community. Similarly, wilderness areas are parts of larger biosystems whose connections can be beneficial to all elements within the system.

Wilderness experiences enhance a sense of family. Strong family units are critical to the health of the planet, and wilderness strengthens these family bonds. When members of a family participate together in wilderness experiences, they grow closer.

A commitment is made to advance wilderness priorities. Each person can influence the advancement of wilderness values. The willingness and spirit to do so is critical to the future well-being of the earth.

With no more frontiers left on a planet where gases from mankind's machines and developments are altering weather patterns with potentially catastrophic results, and with the ongoing growth in the world's population, the time is long overdue to make the values of wilderness, not those of the frontier, the standards that guide civilizations. Just as the spotted owl stands as an umbrella species whose well-being signals the well-being of an old growth forest and the hundreds of other species dependent on this unique environment, so too does the presence of wilderness manifests the health of the earth.

In his pivotal work, *A Sand County Almanac*, Aldo Leopold called for the adoption of a "land ethic." He wrote that a land ethic "changes the role of *Homo sapiens* from conqueror of the land-community to plain member and citizen of it." My pursuit of wild trout has taught me that I must be a respectful citizen of a wilderness community, one who lives by its underlying values. It has taught me that I need to do my part in protecting these precious wild fish, the places where they exist, and all of the other creatures that co-exist with them in a precarious balance.

It was William O. Douglas who captured the essence of wilderness values when he wrote:

> **Only when there is a wilderness, can man harmonize his inner being with the wave lengths of the earth. When the earth, its products, its creatures become his concern, man is caught up in a cause greater than his own life and more meaningful. Only when man loses himself in an endeavor of that magnitude does he walk and live with humility and reverence.**

Epilogue

Many years have passed since that first family trip to the Mokelumne Wilderness. Jennifer, Kirk and Doug have long been on their own as young adults. I've retired from public education, Diane from her position at Stanford Hospital. We sold our Bay Area house, and traded our vacation cabin on Ebbetts Pass for one in the June Lake Loop. We now live in a home on the banks of the Lower Sacramento River in northern California. If I see a nice fish jump while I'm looking out one of our windows, or from our deck, I'm able to grab my rod, go down to the river, and cast to it.

The river and its trout are what first attracted me here. They both are special. The river is always cold, the insects plentiful, the trout fat and healthy. With the large volume of water in the Sacramento, the population of rainbows throughout are wilderness trout in every sense. I live in a fisherman's paradise. But it's more than that, much more.

Not too distant are magnificent mountains for hiking, something Diane and I do regularly, she more than I. Waterfowl by the thousands entertain us all year long. Resident ospreys are my co-fishers. So too are Great Blue herons, Great White egrets, megansers, and river otters by the score, always a delight to observe, except when they invade my fishing space. Canada geese serenade me often with their honking rhapsodies as they zoom past me into the setting sun.

A major rapid dominates the river off of our property. Its constant churning, thrashing tempo blots out all other sounds. Open our bedroom slider and the river sings to us all night long, passing on its message. What I found in those hard-to-get-to places on the Stanislaus, the Tuolumne, the Mokelumne, the East Carson, the San Joaquin, places I sometimes return to, are present here, perhaps in slightly different guises, but here nonetheless. I am where I want and need to be, alongside a river. I am a lucky person.

Appendix

Laws and Programs that Protect Wild Trout

The organizations, governmental laws and programs most instrumental in protecting wild trout are:

- *National Parks.* The first national park was Yellowstone National Park, established in 1872. President Theodore Roosevelt placed national parks under the newly formed National Park Service in 1916. By law the purpose of the park system is the preservation and enjoyment of "the natural and historic objects and the wild life therein," leaving them "unimpaired for the enjoyment of future generations." The National Park Service is now emphasizing the natural functioning of the biosystems within the parks, and preserving the native flora and fauna, with less priority being given to the parks as recreational areas. For example, park waters are no longer stocked with fish, allowing them to return to wild fisheries (or empty of fish). Many of the nation's best wild trout waters are found in national parks which are being viewed more and more as parts of larger ecosystems.

- *Federal Wilderness Act.* The 1964 Federal Wilderness Act created the National Wilderness Preservation System to "secure for the American people of present and future generations the benefits of an enduring resource of wilderness—areas affected primarily by the forces of nature, where the earth and its community of life are untrammeled by man, where man himself is a visitor who does not remain." Among its objectives are: to present outstanding opportunities for solitude or a primitive and unconfined type of recreation; to allow natural ecological processes to operate freely; to maintain watersheds in a healthy condition; and to protect threatened or endangered plant and animal species.

- *National Wild & Scenic Rivers Act.* This 1968 legislation protects rivers and sections of rivers in their free-flowing state primarily by prohibiting new dams and diversions, and by establishing a one-quarter mile corridor on each side of the river to disallow developments and activities harmful to Wild & Scenic values such as roads, logging, and grazing. It is the only status for a river that absolutely protects it from federal hydro licensing.

- *Federal Clean Water Act.* Passed in 1972, this bill's main purpose is to "restore and maintain the chemical, physical, and biological integrity of the Nation's waters." One of its main provisions enforces national standards for "point sources" of pollution—the garbage and poisons flowing into streams and waterways from municipal sewage systems, factories, farms and other sources of contaminants. One of its statutes protects wetlands that are crucial for healthy ecosystems, and which filter "nonpoint" pollution—mostly urban and agriculture runoff.

- *Federal Endangered Species Act.* This 1973 act was established to slow the rate of extinction by singling out animals and plants and giving them special protection. It mandates federal agencies to use the best scientific evidence to list all species in danger of extinction as either "endangered" or "threatened" for these reasons: (1) present or threatened habitat degradation; (2) overutilization for commercial, recreational, scientific, or educational purposes; (3) disease or predation; (4) inadequacy of government regulatory mechanisms; (5) other natural or manmade factors affecting its continued existence. The act requires all federal agencies to ensure actions they authorize, fund or carry out do not jeopardize identified critical habitat of a listed species. The Secretary of the Interior may also identify critical habitat and impose regulations governing these areas. The law prohibits the taking of a species through harassing, harming, pursuing, hunting, shooting, wounding, killing, trapping, capturing, or collecting. It requires the development of a recovery plan that seeks to "delist" the species. In the quarter-century after enactment of the Endangered Species Act, the government has put 1,037 plants and animals under the law's protection. One notable success is the delisting of America's once endangered national bird—the Bald Eagle.

- *The Nature Conservancy.* The mission of this non-profit, publicly-supported private organization is "to preserve plants, animals and natural communities that represent the diversity of life on Earth by protecting the lands and waters they need to survive." One of The Nature Conservancys acquisitions is a section of the McCloud River and its surrounding canyon in northern California. The McCloud is one of the state's blue ribbon trout waters, and is managed by the Conservancy as a wild trout fishery.

In California:

- *California Wild & Scenic Rivers System.* Passed in 1972, this state legislation provides some protections for rivers up to their high water line.

- *California Wild Trout Program.* This state program is designed to maximize wild trout angling opportunities by eliminating stocking of hatchery trout in the selected waters, and by restricting the methods used and the number of fish allowed to be kept—in some cases-zero.

SELECTED SOURCES

1. The Mokelumne Wilderness.
> Johnson, Verna. *California Forests and Woodlands, A Natural History*, University of California Press, 1994.

2. New Zealand.
> Forrester, Rex. *Trout Fishing in New Zealand*, Madrona Publishers, Inc., 1979.
> Sinclair, Keith. *A History of New Zealand*, Penguin Books, 1991.

3. Small Streams.
> Heffernan, Rick. "A Beetles Reunion," In *Backpacker*, December, 1994.

4. The Stanislaus.
> Palmer, Tim. *Stanislaus: The Struggle For A River*, University of California Press, 1982.
> Palmer, Tim. *The Sierra Nevada*, Island Press, 1988.

5. The Tuolumne.
> Cassidy, John. *A Guide toThree Rivers: The Stanislaus, Tuolumne and South Fork of the American*, Friends of the River, 1981.
> Hesse, Herman. *Siddartha*, New Directions Publications, 1951.
> Wright, Terry. *Rocks and Rapids of the Tuolumne River*, A Wilderness Interpretation Publication, 1983.

6. The East Carson.
> Cassady, Jim & Calhoun, Fryar. *California Whitewater*. North Fork Press, 1990.
> Murphy, Shane. *The Lore & Legend of the East Fork*. The Carson River Conservation Fund, 1982.

7. The San Joaquin.
Schullery, Paul and Varley, John D. "Fires and Fish: The Fate of Yellowstone Waters Since 1988," in *TROUT*, Spring, 1994.

8. Fly Fishing Nuances.
Cutter, Ralph. *Sierra Trout Guide.* Frank Amato Publications, 1991.
Hill, Les & Marshall, Graeme. *Stalking Trout.* The Halcyon Press, 1992
White, Ray J. "We're Going Wild," in *TROUT*, 30 year anniversary issue.
White, Ray J. "Why Wild Fish Matter," in *TROUT*, Summer and Autumn issues, 1992.

9. Wilderness Preparation.
Fish, Peter. "It's rattlesnake season again." in *Sunset*, June, 1994
Jenkins, Mark. "What's in the water?" in *Backpacker*, December 1996.
Klauber, Laurence M. *Rattlesnakes. Their Habits, Life Histories, & Influence on Mankind,* University of California Press, 1982.
Rennicke, Jeff. "Swords from the Sky." in *Backpacker*, August, 1994.

10. Preserving Wild Trout
Bass, Rick. "Through Rosalind's Eyes," in *AUDUBON*, July-August, 1996.
California's Rivers: A Public Trust Report, Prepared for the California State Lands Commission, 1993.
Cramer, Jerome. "The Invisible Menace," in *TROUT*, Summer, 1994.
Howe, Steve and Rennicke, Jeff. "People underestimate the power they wield," in *Backpacker*, September, 1996.
Kinch, John A. "Love of Life," in *Nature Conservancy*, March/April, 1996.
Lassila, Kathrin Day. Editorial: "Happy 25th birthday, Clean Water Act," in *The Amicus Journal*, Fall 1997.

Margolis, Jon. "With Solitude for All," in *AUDUBON*, July-August, 1997

Watkins, T.H. "Wilderness and Community," in *The Wilderness Year*, 1996.

Williams, Ted. "Deregulating the Wild," in *AUDUBON*, July-August, 1997.

Williams, Ted. "Defense of the Realm," in *SIERRA*, January/February 1996.

Index

Fish And Game, 73, 91, 111, 154
California Fish And Game Commission, 92
California Scenic Rivers System, 60, 111, 178
California Wild Trout Program, 92, 178
California Wilderness Act, 12, 76, 114
Caltrout, , 92, 170
Camp Irene, 11, 13, 16, 20
Camp Irene Trail, 13
Camp Nine, 53, 55-6, 61, 63
Canada geese, 175
Cancer, basal cell, 88-9
Cancer, squamish cell, 88-9
Canterbury Plains (N.Z.), 28
Caroline Bay (N.Z.), 29
Carson, Kit, 12, 95
Carson Pass, 11
Carson Sink, 95
Carson-Iceberg Wilderness, 95
Carter, Jimmy, 60-1
Cedar tree, 16, 20
Cedar Camp, 11, 20
Cellular phone, 150
Chalk stream, 163
Chamberlain, Richard, 75-6
Channelization, 160
Chief Seattle, 113
Chinese Camp, 83
Chiseling of stream banks, 159
Christchurch (N.Z.), 27-8, 36
Civilian Conservation Corps, 20, 72
Clavey Falls, 71, 91
Clean Water Act, 177
Coelho, Tony (Congressman), 73
Coho salmon, 165
Complex forest, 164-5
Comstock Lode, 96

Community, 10, 93, 172
Connecticut, 9, 15, 145
Conservationists, 169
Constriction Band, 154
Convergent "Lady Bird" Beetles, 50
Cook's Strait (N.Z.), 27-8
Cows (cattle), 72, 111, 159
Coyote, 70, 84, 106
CPR (Cardiovascular Pulmonary Respiration), 152
Cranston, Senator Alan, 76
Crested meganser duck, 78
Cryptosporidium, 148
Culture, 162
Cumulous clouds, 17
Cutter, Ralph, 99, 100, 101, 140
Cutthroat trout, 163

Dams and diversions, 56-8, 159
Deer, 70
Dehydration, 148
Detritus, 164
Devil's Postpile National Monument, 113-117, 127
Dinghy, 56-8, 86
Don Pedro Dam, 69
Douglas, William O., 173
Dragon flies, 79
Dried fruit, 15, 82
Dubois, Mark, 60
Duct tape, 149
Dunsmuir, 159

Eagle Lake, 164
Eagles, 70, 163
East Carson Hot Springs, 96
East Carson River, 95-112
East Walker River, 136, 157
Ebbetts Pass, 11, 54, 96, 99
Ecosystem, 129, 161-167
Edmundson, Jim, 92

To order more copies of *Pursuing Wild Trout*

Send $14.95 per copy ordered, plus $3.00 for shipping (up to two books—First Class Priority mailing). After two books, add $1.00 for each additional book. Please add the sales tax of 7.75% ($1.15 per book) for books shipped to a California address.

An 11" x 14" print of the picture, *Forest Guardian*, on page 168, suitable for framing, is available for $19.95 (includes shipping). Please add the sales tax of 7.75% ($1.55) for a print shipped to a California address.

Send your order (checks only) to:
River Bend Books—Suite A
6412 Clear View Dr.
Anderson, CA. 96007
(530) 365-5852